thonik®

BIS Publishers, Amsterdam 2001

BIS Publishers
Nieuwe Spiegelstraat 36
1017 DG Amsterdam
The Netherlands
T 020-620 51 71
F 020-627 92 51
bis@bispublishers.nl
www.bispublishers.nl

ISBN 90-72007-87-5

Contents

Ed van Hinte

ThNi CoOp

Thonik was still called Gonnissen and Widdershoven when I first worked with them. As a member of the board of the Eternally Yours foundation I acted as commissioner. Later on I also assumed the role of co-designer and commissioner, because cooperation came naturally to us.

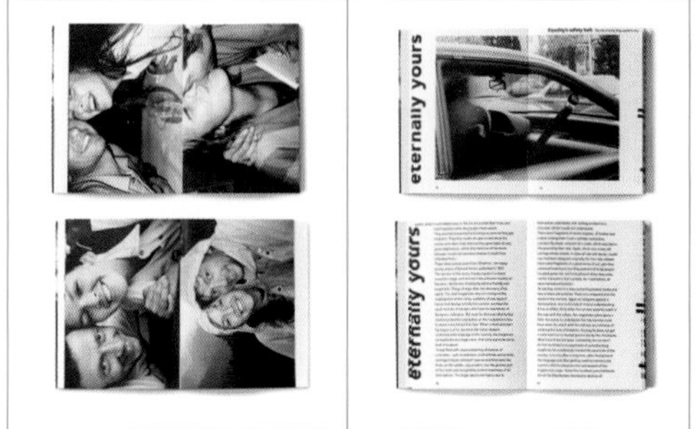

Eternally Yours, p. 110

Eternally Yours and De Volkskrant Opmaat supplement, p. 112

Eternally Yours, congress invitation

For me, the Eternally Yours print project was a fast learning experience in graphic design, and great fun too. Eternally Yours, a foundation which I co-founded to investigate product life-span extension, was preparing its first congress in 1997. Gonnissen and Widdershoven seemed a good choice for the invitation and the congress information, although I knew very little about them. As a journalist with a background in industrial design I considered graphic design quite separate. I had some ideas, though, especially about the format of the congress information. Having attended numerous conferences I knew that you usually got a stack of horribly printed paper, sometimes in a plastic folder or a cheap quasi attaché case, with a superfluous ballpoint pen. As if congress visitors still have to learn how to write.

I decided on simplicity and suggested that all we really needed was a notepad with programme information preprinted on the first fifteen pages. Thomas liked this idea, but he and his partner Nikki still managed to surprise the Eternally Yours team with their design: a pad with a gold cover symbolising a wedding ring and inside, amorous pictures of themselves. At first I was slightly confused. I didn't know about Thomas and Nikki's crusade against the label 'new austerity' that their earlier work had acquired – which was why they used their own pictures in their designs.

There were as many as twenty images of the lovers in the pad. But when Thomas said he didn't mind if we reduced the number (a kind of trade-off for the concept) I saw the joke and agreed, after taking out a couple of pictures of course. Otherwise I wouldn't have been much of a negotiator.

The congress invitation completed the ingenuity of the design: an A4 sheet, printed and rolled so that the top half of the title typography 'Eternally Yours' exactly met the bottom half on the paper scroll. It was held together by a brass ring. I remember this was slightly problematic at that time, given Eternally Yours's environmental principles. In the end the ring went ahead since people would keep them and anyway, the number of invitations to be sent out was negligible.

The notepad worked well at the congress, not just because of the design, but the design's implications for the congress content too. I'll never forget the keynote speaker Ezio 'no-congress-is-complete-without-him' Manzini waving it and stating that the idea of an eternal love bond between people and products was nonsense. He was right, and the design helped him make this 'very important' point.

Making the Eternally Yours book after the congress was a special experience. Again Thomas embraced one of my ideas: starting every chapter as a caption with an illustration. Some people find it insulting when others use their ideas. I feel flattered. That's what cooperation is all about. Unused ideas have little value anyway.

Again Gonnissen and Widdershoven surprised us; not with the pictures of Nikki and Thomas – we were used to them by now – but with the small size and gilt-edging, the beautiful and warm title appearing through the pages. Gonnissen and Widdershoven's book gave me a fresh perspective on images. It contains a picture of a red car; when we discussed which illustrations should be in black and white and which in full colour, Thomas said it would be nice to have this 'red smear' in between black and white pages. I realised then that figurative images are also abstract. It's about keeping an open mind for images. A similar phenomenon: Thomas and Nikki portrayed themselves on the cover, upside down. It's a flowing image that confuses people, they are unclear which way up the book should be. It more or less forces them to choose abstraction.

ƎD VAN HINTE
Leyweg 627
PO box 43363
2504 AJ The Hague
The Netherlands
e ejhint@wxs.nl
t +31 (0)70 35 95 850
f +31 (0)70 35 95 369

Business card and correspondence card in one

Later on I followed Gonnissen and Widdershoven's work with interest and came to understand more about the idiosyncrasies of graphic design. We became friends and I asked Thomas to do a business card for me which could also serve as a correspondence card. The basic idea came in a half-hour brainstorm. Thomas started folding pieces of paper and I worked out a way of putting my first name at the beginning of the card but at the end of the correspondence card when unfolded.
Meanwhile, Thomas told me he was looking for a new name for his studio. His first idea was Orange Office, emphasising his Dutchness, but specialists advised him against this since colours are difficult to claim, especially orange in Holland. Some mediocre proposals followed and then, after a long night of thinking I suggested using the first three letters of Thomas and Nikki. Thonik looks different, and at the same time the word sounds familiar as a generic term for a restorative drink.

Recently, because of my technical background, I became involved in a Droog Design project: a commission by the San Francisco Museum Of Modern Art to contribute to an exhibition called '010101 Art in Technological Times'. My role was to participate in sessions with selected designers to generate ideas. The most inspirational was Matijs Korpershoek: a mirror, apparently without any special features, that showed images or texts when breathed on.
We needed someone to create an interesting image and chose Thomas, because of his background as a philosopher and his conceptual skills. He came up with a brilliant plan: one breath visualised five centimetres, just enough space for four letters. Four letter words were the business. And since fuck could also be printed f*ck, with * as the visual equivalent of a beep, * was included as an extra vowel. The title became Four letr word – find f*ck face.
Thomas estimated that there were about 5,000 genuine four letter words in English. However, he calculated that since the mirror was 2.4 metres high and 4.8 wide, with enough space for 15,000 words, he needed 10,000 more non-existent words from a possible 80,000 with a minimum of one vowel. He asked if I knew anyone who could draw up a list. I said that I could do the job myself; the problem seemed rather intriguing.

SFMoma installation view, p. 88

SFMoma installation view, p. 90

So we bought an expensive electronic English dictionary, only to discover that we couldn't extract the four letter words automatically. Luckily a complete word list was available on Internet. For the non-existent words I discovered that Thomas had underestimated the number of possibilities by a factor of 4.5. The random selection had to be extracted from some 350,000 combinations. It took me and my computer two days.
Meanwhile, Lauran Schijvens conceived the idea of initiating activities using the barcodes that people carry around unawares. The object being to demonstrate that it is easy, and confusing, to transfer codes or information from one context to another: 'system almighty' –

SFMoma installation view

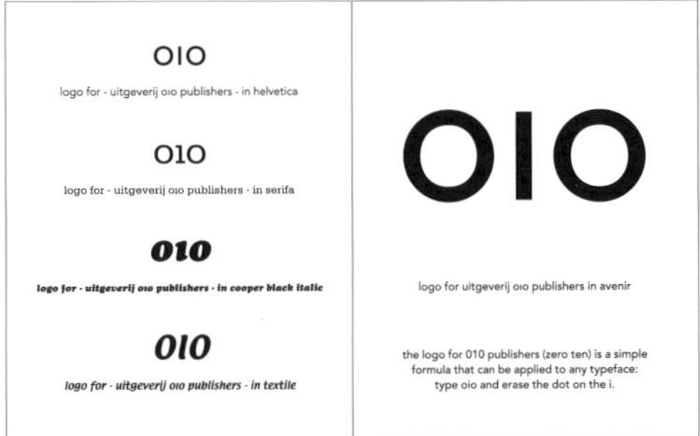

Logo for 010 publishers, p. 94

a well-chosen title by Renny Ramakers. One of the ideas Thomas discussed was to allow each barcode to start a combination of electric products, some by Droog Design, others bought in hardware shops and second hand stores. He became enthusiastic and accepted the commission to create this noisy installation himself. It wasn't really his thing, though. So he called me in to help. Together we found a way to make a convincing and simple presentation. 'Scan barcode here'. And that's what people did. They searched their pockets and bags for things with barcodes and stood in line at the scanner. Favourites were saws, synthesisers and electric trains.

I was recently reappointed commissioner, as editor and publisher for 010 press in Rotterdam. We needed a new corporate style, not to create a sense of uniformity or a particular type for all our books, but rather of a kind of order and functional simplicity combined with the freedom to digress. We agreed that 010 was a good name and logo, whatever the letter type. Thomas still managed to surprise us. He suggested that there was a unique way to print 010 in any font by printing lower case 'oio', but without the dot on the i. It was the first time I ever saw a logo created by rubbing out a dot.

Ineke Schwartz

Away with Form

An interview with Nikki Gonnissen and Thomas Widdershoven

Gonnissen and Widdershoven: Original and Innovative
They are mentioned no less than three times in leading American magazine I-D's annual international design charts: Nikki Gonnissen (b. 1967) and Thomas Widdershoven (b. 1960). Having studied philosophy, Widdershoven continued with graphic design at Rietveld Academy, Gonnissen at Utrecht's Hogeschool voor de Kunsten. They are the most original and innovative young designers around at present. Partners in life and work. Created a stir recently by featuring their own pictures in their designs. For Eternally Yours, a book on sustainable product development, they used their love life as a metaphor; the cover shows their first kiss. Their style is impossible to pigeonhole. An ingenious creation was the superimposition of red and green English and Dutch texts in a Wim T. Schippers catalogue, to be read using the enclosed filter.

From an article about Dutch Design by Ineke Schwartz in Elsevier Magazine, no. 38, 19 September 1998

The Best of Wim T. Schippers catalogue, p. 60

Thonik's new studio in Amsterdam, designed by MVRDV, p. 86

Parool newspaper as a change of address notice

Thonik

How do you reduce a commission to a single principle? How do you shape a design as little as possible? How do you pursue a single idea as explicitly and consistently as possible? How do you strip a briefing down to the bone and then return it to the client as precisely the solution that they asked for?
Those are typical Thonik questions. The answers are in their work. How Thonik's work, and those answers materialise is not always clear to the outsider. That is what this article is about, based on a series of interviews with the designers. Quotations are in cyan.

Nikki Gonnissen and Thomas Widdershoven have lived and worked together since 1993: first as Studio Gonnissen and Widdershoven and since 2000 as Thonik. Their mission: to conquer the world with a conceptual form of graphic design. Without style and with a minimum of form. But employing a number of central models or themes that constantly reappear and turn each work, however unpredictably, turning each into a recognisable Thonik.
So what is Thonik? It's using your own love life as a metaphor for a book about sustainable product development – with a photo of your first kiss on the cover (Eternally Yours, 1997). It's superimposing the English and Dutch texts in red and green in the second catalogue of a rebellious Fluxus artist, so that they can only be read with the enclosed colour filter (Het beste van/The best of Wim T. Schippers, 1997). And if the commotion surrounding the bright orange colour of your new studio hits the press, buying up hundreds of newspapers carrying the story on the front page, adding address labels and sending them to your friends as a change of address notice. That's Thonik.

Style or not, their work is gradually beginning to acquire a recognisable quality. All the activities of Nikki Gonnissen, Thomas Widdershoven and their agency contribute to the impact of the Thonik name. Either intentionally or unintentionally. The commissions, the solutions, the commotion surrounding the new studio, their television appearances. The ideas that are central to their lives and their work, are the foundation: concept, order, minimalism, personality, art books, stories, recycling, brand. What emerges is what Thonik call their design principle: if the concept is good, the rest follows naturally.

Concept

Thonik's design principles and methods differ from that of other graphic designers. In fact they are more like artists and architects. Instead of allowing clients to state what they want, it's they who tell the client. They like nothing better than to solve problems for them. The tougher the problem the more fun, and the better Thonik's work. The more stumbling blocks, the clearer the result. A question of consistent analysis: Thonik dissect commissions down to the bone, reduce them to a clear principle and at the planning presentation serve them back to the client, with the solution. It's reminiscent of Rem Koolhaas's method, who raised research, analysis and stylelessness to the essential ingredients of the design process. Without a briefing, Thonik establish their own boundaries to attack. Even designs that consist of various layers are based on a single principle. That one idea, expressed in the term 'concept' that Thonik love using, is what it's all about. Once the concept has been decided, the main work is done. The execution is actually boring. The concept is implemented to its extreme logical conclusion, radically and mechanically. Aesthetics, form and the usual concern with letter types and layout hardly play a role. Thonik employ standard formats, a basic, no-nonsense design and one type: Avenir. That the result is also always a commentary on graphic design itself is an additional aspect that actually forms part of Thonik's basic principle.

From the start Thonik have been at the forefront of a new generation of graphic designers who are searching in yet another age of change for a new role – with even less servility than ever. The designer as director, as conceptual artist, as strategist, as media expert and as obstinate busybody – Thonik cover all these roles with gusto. And with results.
It's a remarkable approach: to do your own thing within the parameters of someone else's assignment. To be a conceptual artist working on a commission. It fits in well with today's discernable shift in art. Until recently, designers admired artists for their autonomy; now they seem to have the advantage, contributing in a major way to visual culture and in touch with the public. Because whatever graphic designers create, their print work, websites, magazines, flyers, strategies and other communication forms (Thonik recently developed an exhibition of Japanese fashion for the Centraal Museum in Utrecht) are guaranteed to reach thousands of people.
Perhaps Thonik's approach is the ultimate interpretation of applied art in the new, positive sense: headstrong about substance and principle, and never without an audience. In Holland's design climate, where books on art and culture are government subsidised and can appear in small, exclusive print runs, this remarkable attitude has been able to blossom and flourish.

Japanese fashion exhibition, Made in Japan, p. 142

For them, working with concepts was a way of jettisoning constraints such as style and form. Especially that highly personal style and form and the artificial involvement preached to students at academies by teachers who had been young in the sixties and seventies and who hoped to carry the torch of Holland's glorious tradition of graphic design.
Thonik (then still Gonnissen en Widdershoven) wanted to get away from graphic design as personal expression and preferred logic and intuition to style and taste. Intuition as understood by artists like John Cage and Sol LeWitt: a force that helps eradicate personal taste through overwhelming sensibility. Logic as medium for analysis and a way of consistently executing intuition. Precisely Sol LeWitt's fifth creed: 'Irrational thoughts should be followed absolutely and logically'.[1]

1 Sol Lewitt, Sentences on Conceptual Art. First published in the 0-9 Archive (a collection of correspondence and manuscripts sent to the editors Vito Hannibal Acconci and Bernadette Meyer 1967-69), Fales Library/Special Collections, New York University; www.altx.com/vizarts/conceptual.html

Not that this had all been thought up in advance. The work was always there, the reflection came later. First you realise you keep making the same choices, that you're searching for standard formats and for that same letter type yet again. Then that becomes a principle and later a reason to do the same again – quite shamelessly.

One size fits all, p. 58

Stories

Thonik, Concept, Art books, Recycling, One size fits all or Avenir – for Thonik these are all titles of stories that define the parameters of their work. Large and small stories, contrived but essential to discover Thonik's consistency and coherence. Their own stepping stones to

The Best Book Designs catalogue, p. 74

escape from the visual soup of postmodernism and the unwritten rules of graphic design. No absolute truths, just thoughts and observations that they keep as long as they believe in them. Ideas that you toy with for a while, that you repeat, change, adapt, use and eventually drop. Thonik's use of 'concept' actually represents a context. They formulate it as follows:
The great thing about a good concept is that it has a minimal amount of form, it reveals itself and results in a double sensation. That's what happens when a person sees a conceptual work. A visual stimulus excites a mental stimulus, the viewer suspects a certain logic but can't find it yet, the brain produces serotonine, analyses, understands more, and finally gets it – bingo! Even more serotonine! It's a way of reaching people that's active and highly rewarding.

KesselsKramer book, p. 128

Each project has its own story which fits into a framework. Recycling is one context for stories. It means turning existing print work into new print work, or recycling Thonik's own ideas. They first used pages from existing books in de 50 Best Verzorgde Boeken (The Best Book Designs) catalogue. Thonik produced a parody of this in KesselsKramer's book of 50 different, fictive covers. In the monthly folders for De Balie, a political and cultural centre, the idea of recycling acquired an entirely new content with an added ingredient: the cover features three superimposed forms, each replaced alternately every fourth issue, presenting a successively changing image.

De Balie identity programme and magazine, p. 118

'Five collections, one museum' is one of Thonik's favourite stories. Centraal Museum wanted a greater sense of unity in their presentation. With all their different activities they had lost that sense of identity. How to turn diversity into unity?
Thonik devised a logo based on five Cs, grouped like the dots of the five on dice. A calm, comprehensible form offering plenty of opportunity for new stories. Each C represents a curator and a part of the collection. The overall image focuses powerfully on the centre and resembles a medieval heraldic symbol. It's a kind of stamp, a minimalist version of a house style which can be applied anywhere. Any image, any style and any ambience can be brought under the Centraal Museum umbrella by simply printing the five Cs over it. And they take chances with it too, who ever heard of anyone brazenly plastering their logo across all their print work?
Maintaining simplicity creates space. Space that can be used in all sorts of ways. That is the real message of this Thonik story. Most house styles are accompanied by manuals with rules carved in stone. 'Five collections, One museum' is a simple basic structure which is strong enough to remain recognisable and flexible enough to join in at every level. It's like playing chess with only a few pieces: all the previous moves echo in every step Thonik make.
Meanwhile, Centraal Museum has become a brand. Playing with the C is part of their identity. You could call it a strategy, but Thonik prefer to see it as a story.

Centraal Museum logo, p. 22

Art books

Art books are another story – and a hard and fast Thonik principle. An art book is only an art book if it functions as an autonomous work by the artist. Sometimes the artist has to be persuaded to accept the idea: Thonik don't make 'ordinary' catalogues with illustrations around a narrative.

2 Richard Prince, Spiritual America, IVAM (Instituto Valenciano de Arte Moderno), 1989

A turning point for Thonik was the exhibition catalogue of American artist Richard Prince,[2] who presented a show at Boijmans Van Beuningen Museum in Rotterdam in 1993, the year Thomas and Nikki gratuaded. For Prince, who transformed photographic icons from popular culture into paintings and sculpture, the catalogue was a natural extension of his work. Fascinated by the paradox of presentation and representation, Thonik tried to resolve this in their own art books. They succeeded brilliantly in N.T.Z.T. (Narcisse Tordoir Zonder Titel – Untitled, 1997). This book, which accompanied a retrospective on this Belgian artist, contains examples of Tordoir's abstract drawings, as well as illustrations of the exhibited works; occasionally they even added a photo showing the source of Tordoir's inspiration. As a result, the book presents the artist's work, instead of presenting reproductions of his work. In fact the presentation in the book is even better than the presentation in the gallery. The museum gratefully adopted Thonik's title N.T.Z.T for the show. A complex paradox – it could hardly get more intricate.

N.T.Z.T. (Narcisse Tordoir Zonder Titel), p. 134

Personal

Another story with various subplots is 'personal'. Why use your own picture on the cover of a book? There are several reasons.

It started as a logical consequence of Thonik's standard formula: the result of an analysis of a briefing for the Nederlandse Raad voor Cultuur (Dutch Culture Council) annual report. Every year the Raad invites a different designer to develop the report, which only works if designers are able to present their style. But Thonik have no style. Besides the design had to be very free – which is not easy if you usually base your approach on an analysis of the briefing.

Another reason was vanity. One year, after returning from a journey to New Guinea, Thonik discovered that all the hip magazines had replaced their usual post-modern mix of styles with an austere, minimalist approach that seemed to reflect Thonik's own work. Superficially, you might have thought Thonik were part of a trend – and that was not what we wanted.

If everything was to be cool, sober and distanced, they decided to become warmer and more personal. But in our own way: not with typography but by including ourselves in the design.

So the Raad voor Cultuur annual report was presented with a personal pictorial story of Thonik's holiday among the Papuans. After the holiday snaps came love and the house.

Eternally Yours, a book about developing sustainable products, was decorated with photos charting Thonik's love life. And for a book on Droog Design products Thonik showed photos of chairs, lamps and other objects being moved into their home.

Raad voor Cultuur annual report, Droog Design and Eternally Yours

Eternally Yours and Volkskrant's Opmaat supplement p. 112

The result of this interplay of the conceptual and personal was to make the unusual ordinary and the ordinary unusual. The Droog products acquired a context, the Raad voor Cultuur's work was put into perspective and the notion of sustainability was injected with emotional content. The phenomenon of a designer couple portraying themselves in their own work gained them worldwide noteriety.

It became a hype, which clients began to ask for. That was enough for them. They didn't want an egotrip and certainly not a new style. To break the spell the now pregnant Nikki posed in Thomas's arms on a romantically lit beach for the cover of the entertainment supplement of

Postage stamp design, p. 116

Cor Dera, Guide to Nature catalogue, p. 70

Init, design for a façade, p. 100

Identity programme for Documenta XI, p. 38

Ennu and Onno, a prêt-à-porter shop and a theatre play, p. 136

De Volkskrant newspaper. And to round it off, in 1998 they appeared on their own postage stamp – although unrecognisable under the make up. Time for a new story.

'It's not very attractive, but the idea's good'

A consequence of the Thonik method is that the result is not always aesthetically pleasing. That too is a story: It's not very attractive, but the idea's good.
Sometimes Thonik allow the hegemony of the idea so much leeway that the form begins to suffer; some designs are simply ugly. That goes against every rule of Holland's clean and aesthetic design tradition. Occasionally, the form is so radically reduced that the basic idea behind it is practically lost. That's what happened to the book on the artist Cor Dera. The idea of basing it on an existing nature guide and simply giving it a new cover was revolutionary and fitted in perfectly with Dera, who reuses nature pictures. At once supportive and autonomous, Thonik's design is a gem of a statement and a commentary on graphic design. It has everything it needs to make it exceptional – except that it's so subtle almost no one realises.

Brands

The latest story is about brands – and about the Thonik brand itself. After years of having denied the existence of a style, claiming Thonik worked purely with concepts, that every form emerged from the concept and that we were chameleons who took our clients' perspective, now there seems to be a style after all. Quite a definite style even. The recurring themes are what define a Thonik work. Which is fortunate, because Thonik are increasingly experimenting with projects that can hardly be called graphic design any more, like media strategy, a character for a theatre performance or the façade of a modern building.

Brand mentality has been on the cards for a while. The five Cs at Centraal Museum established the institution as a brand. A key move was the Documenta XI logo. Thonik was commissioned to devise a logo for the largest European contemporary art event by Droog Design. Their loathing for house styles and logos led them to propose both a medium and a strategy for the exhibition: a T-shirt with two upturned exclamation marks as the Documenta logo. Again a simple and open structure which could then be toyed with: ii is eleven; it can also be an abstract symbol, two equal people, a man and a woman and probably much more besides. For those who know, it also means Documenta XI. Everyone in the world wearing the T-shirt is part of the event, whether consciously or not. So people carry the logo and a design becomes a media strategy to be taken as far as the client wishes. As a preview, Thonik sent shirts to friends around the world, who sent back photos of themselves as Documenta logo carriers.

The Documenta proposal wasn't taken up, but the concept was good and it was developed further: first Onno, the anonymous figure developed for Dogtroep theatre company, then Ennu ('and now') the shop idea, and Thonik themselves – the name that reflects their dual identity and at last gives them a handle foreigners can pronounce. Maximum substance and minimum form are linked in the most basic of ways: Thonik have become a concept.

Gert Staal

A Love Affair of Poetry and Trash

A brand in the Dutch design world

De Zingende Zaag, poetry magazine, p. 20

Raad voor Cultuur annual report, p. 102

Eternally Yours and Volkskrant's Opmaat supplement, p. 112

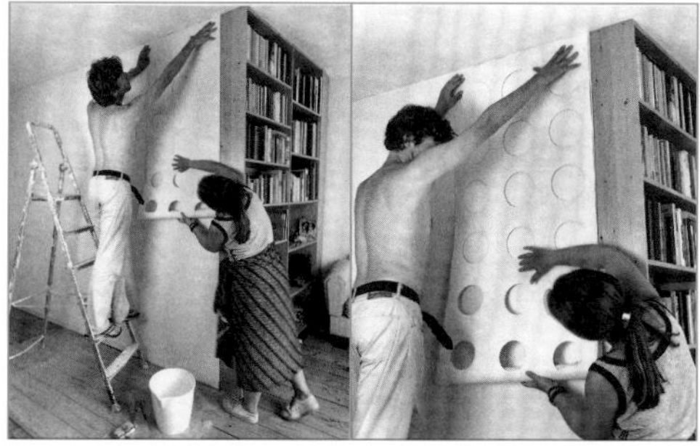

Droog Design 1991-1996 catalogue, p. 106

A combination of surnames changed in the course of 2000 into a concurrence of first names. Studio Gonnissen and Widdershoven – for years an established name on the print work produced for Utrecht's Centraal Museum, De Zingende Zaag poetry magazine and numerous other clients – reemerged as Thonik: Thomas and Nikki, joined in symbiotic unity. A mere nominal shift? Or was it more?

Thomas and Nikki, who regularly appeared in their own work in the late 1990s, have moved on since 2000 to become proponents of almost abstract brands. In the Raad voor Cultuur annual report (1996) they appeared among the Asmat peoples of Papua New Guinea; for De Volkskrant Opmaat supplement (1998) they posed against the light on the Dutch coast, full page; and they visualised the theme for the Eternally Yours design conference (1997) – where the discussion focused on longterm loyalty to consumer products as an alternative to mindless disposable consumption – in a series of designs based on the love of a man and a woman: this man and this woman, to be precise.

The conference invitation was rolled up and held in place with a wedding ring. And when the conference report was bundled in a book, the designers again illustrated it with their own relationship. An abstraction from the theme, but such a direct expression of the ambitions enshrined in Eternally Yours that no one could ever accuse the makers of this much-lauded book of being narcissists or poseurs.

The modest format, the black-and-white illustrations: every possible means was employed to lend a sense of authenticity. Only the cut edge of the book was gilded, with the title legible. Reality was represented as naturally as possible; the dream resting like a film over the pages.

For the Droog Design publication (Centraal Museum, Utrecht 1997) they shipped an entire arsenal of furniture and accessories by the designers to their house in the Amsterdam Pijp area. Cupboards were placed in the house, mirrors fixed, a sofa was hoisted up by the beam, wallpaper pasted. The snapshots of the day's events replaced the cold product photos that normally illustrate that kind of book. Blood, sweat and tears instead of perfect settings, directed by a news photographer and printed in black and white like any decent news picture. By using interpretative images the designers showed what the Droog Design collection actually is: an assembly of furniture made to be used. Strange as it may seem, this was the first time that this much-vaunted initiative had been taken out of its museum context and returned to the everyday surroundings which had inspired it. The visible presence of the graphic designers in the book is the logical conclusion of the line of reasoning they followed.

The self portraits are no longer part of their work. They represent a phase in Nikki Gonnissen and Thomas Widdershoven's oeuvre in which they searched for visible personal involvement. They may have had every reason to do so, not because their work lacked conviction in any way, but to force a breakthrough. For them, these self portraits represented a crucial antidote to the cool abstraction into which their designs had gradually descended. Commissions were reduced to their very core resulting almost in plain propositions. Gonnissen and Widdershoven's books, posters and to a lesser extent their magazines exploited the purity of a single idea by taking it to every logical conclusion. The result being the unavoidable outcome of a train of thought, not the stylisation of a fashion or aesthetic ideal. Whatever the result, wherever reason led was acceptable. Even if it could subjectively be considered

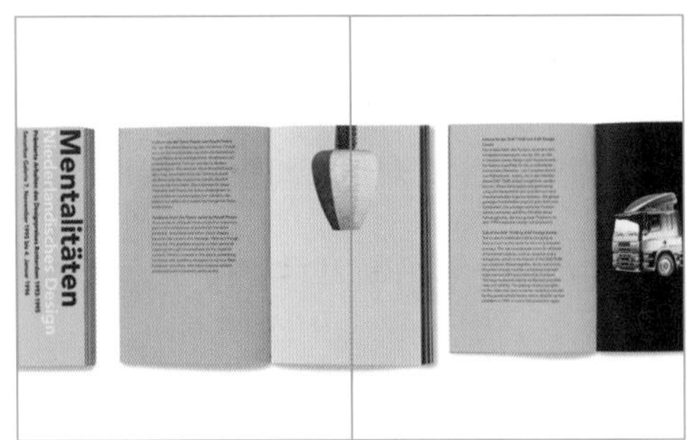

Mentalitäten catalogue, p. 76

Ennu and Onno, a prêt-à-porter shop and a theatre play, p. 136

n8, name and identity programme for the Amsterdam museum night and 1ab, name and identity programme for the first architecture biennial in Rotterdam, p. 138

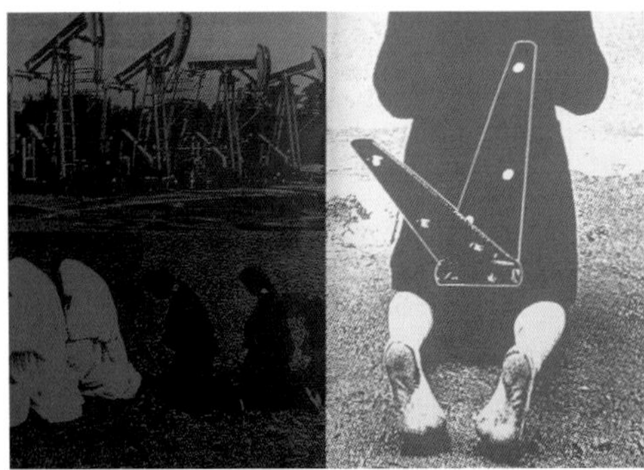

De Knie, exam project of Nikki Gonnissen

unattractive – although their designer's heart often persuaded them to avoid the furthest of extremes.

Frequently, these ideas came about through restrictions. Limited budgets forced them to use simpler materials, which in turn influenced the development of the concept. For example, the most significant adjustment to the Mentalitäten exhibition catalogue for the Rotterdam Kunststichting and Dutch Design Institute (1996), was the colour scheme applied with almost mathematical consistency as the background on all the photo pages. Two colours were distributed in a predetermined system of proportions throughout the book. Mixed at hundred per cent, the colours were practically black; other combinations resulted in a pallette ranging from green to brown to purple. By cutting the edge of the book diagonally they ensured that all the tones would be visible when the book was closed. But that wasn't enough for the designers. They added a passage in the colophon explaining the system, impressing upon the reader the importance of the concept and the added value that this gave to the publication. It's a modest but characteristic illustration of Gonnissen and Widdershoven's search in this period. While they felt a need to justify their treatment of materials – like a footnote in a scientific report – their comments encouraged the reader to look more closely, to an extent even to empathise with the designers. The neutral system was intended to excite a personal response from the reader or at least to make the reader part of the design idea.

An immediately striking parallel is their name change. This too is a realignment of the neutral and the personal. Their original name was an abstraction, not suggesting in any way what it was that they did – they could have been lawyers, bookkeepers, glaziers. It gradually forced them to make their work more personal. So when the self portraits came to end, the studio had to become more like a brand and take on an artificial identity.

Thonik became a conduit for a design approach closely linked to the notion of identity; that of designers and clients alike. Even more than in recent years, that identity has become the subject of the design. Thonik created Onno for Dogtroep, Ennu (and now) for a high-street clothes shop and n8 (night) for a nocturnal museum event. The designs are less concerned with defining the message than with creating communicative space. Increasingly, perfectly contrived end products have made way for models that allow a broad range of interpretation and transformation during their lifetime. The form is drawn from the practical circumstances: n8 offered a magical view of the city at night on a picture postcard, but the poster and the website for the same event shows the name simply as a typographic symbol.

In these cases design is more like a strategic operation. The images develop alongside the identity that the designers specifically attach to them, or which the clients provide as the basic principle. Much of Thonik's recent work falls under the first category, although sometimes their powers of persuasion ensure that space is found for a reformulation of the assignment.

Museum director Jan Hoet invited Gonnissen and Widdershoven to Gent after seeing Nikki Gonnissen's exam project at Plaatsmaken publishers. He needed no persuading for the graphic image for his Over the Edges show (2000). Having become familiar with their work convinced him not to make his choice dependent on their presentation. This loyalty remained and led in 2001 to their collaboration on the Sonsbeek project, which Hoet curated.

Over the Edges placed work by artists from different countries in open spaces, streets and

Over the Edges, visual communication for an art event, p. 54

Sonsbeek 9, visual communication for an art event, p. 124

squares of the city of Ghent. The event's identity could not be linked to a specific work or artist – the participants were too disparate. Its diversity made it impossible to turn the actual city into a symbol. And since they decided not to focus on the curator as a person, only one option remained for an umbrella concept. Which is why Thonik adopted Hoet's title for a typographical play on words in the posters, the catalogue and the television commercial.
The text image of Over the Edges appeared on all the publicity. Dominated everywhere by the capital E – cut into the cardboard case of the catalogue, for example, or filling the whole space like a monumental structure on the posters. The idea was brutally simple, yet opened the door to a series of posters some of which cited the entire title, while others used only part: down to the red poster with only the four Es remaining, combined with the E from the city's name. Despite the abstraction, the images remained recognisable as posters for the event, which might literally be taking place on the adjoining square. The colours were simple, yet through consistent use they remained signals; the positions and size of the letters stayed the same and contributed to the recognisablility of what might otherwise have been a completely unrelated message. In the end, five Es were enough to tell the story. The abstraction was arranged so carefully that no one in Ghent could have been confused.

Over the years, the studio's work has increasingly acquired the reputation of being 'conceptual'. A word that is appallingly abused and often merely indicates that the design has been thought about. Half Dutch Design is conceptual if we're to believe the discussions and brochures. Sometimes, however, the term is accurate. Unfortunately, there is no uncontaminated phrase to precisely describe what makes Nikki Gonnissen and Thomas Widdershoven's work so powerful: namely their ability to analyse an assignment, to focus the perspective and so create more space for interpretation. Parsimony and restriction are used to give a single idea the power of a hurricane and the agility of a spring breeze.
The conscious search for accuracy begins long before the first computer sketches are made. Reflection visibly precedes action. Only when an idea is sufficiently watertight is it given shape. As little shape as possible ... A single letter type – Avenir – suffices for almost every publication. In that sense Thonik are quite different from most Dutch designers. The value lies in the actual idea. The power of mental agility. Whereas many designers resort to showing their muscles, Thonik prefer a subtle anecdote that sets the tone for a different way of communicating. Hardly surprising that their work has attracted the interest of cultural clients. While designers sometimes have to shout to get the public's attention, Thonik's approach is a breath of fresh air. Intellectual but not intellectualised. Naughty where necessary. And clever, because then you don't need to be strong.

That's the quality that characterises Thonik's work. Behind the formal recognition, lies the attractive power of their books, magazines and posters to open people's eyes and draw them into their world of ideas. Their design has a natural quality but also resists excessively simple consumption. These products aren't made for ease of use, although they play a constant game of seduction – alternately tactile and cerebral. And just when you think you've understood the formula, they move on. Like that intriguing boy who fascinates you throughout primary school but never lets himself be pinned down.

Typically for them, they were immediately hailed by their fellow designers. Like musicians' musicians, Nikki Gonnissen and Thomas Widdershoven are probably first and foremost designers' designers. Designers whose approach to their work changed the ground rules in the profession; to such an extent that people in the trade are already talking about a new style.

That's misleading, however. Thonik are more a state of mind than a style, which is precisely why they attract fewer imitators. Adopting their tools provides only part of the key. Hundreds of pages set in Avenir do not make a Thonik book. The safe where the ideas are stashed is not an easy one to crack.

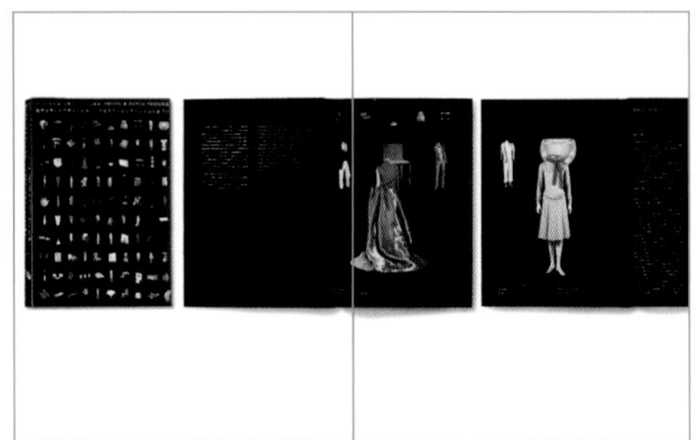

Droog & Dutch Design catalogue, p. 144

Of course, being the focus of the design community, there is also a danger that Thonik's work loses touch with the outside world. That their communication becomes limited to conversations with fellow designers, or even to an interior monologue. In some respects that is perhaps their Achilles heel: the explanation in the Mentalitäten catalogue colophon is an obvious example. It seems like an attempt by the designers to involve the public in considerations which they may indeed have missed, but which are actually none of their concern. Just as readers of Droog & Dutch Design (2000) do not expect to have to digest information about the principles behind Thonik's arrangement of the illustrations. It's the trap into which conceptualism can lead when articulated in text.

Samsam children's magazine

But the damage is not serious. In a magazine like Samsam (1997 to date) and the book Mario ♥ Olimpia (1997) – both commissioned by Amsterdam's Tropical Museum and aimed at young readers – the design is subordinated to the need to spread information. So Samsam was able to feature a visual plethora to which practically all of Thonik's colleagues contributed. An adult children's party. Conceptual control would also have been out of place when the studio worked with artist Roy Villevoye on three publications of the account of his travels to the Asmat. The domination of the designers is nowhere to be found, allowing Villevoye's illustrated story plenty of space to be told.

Mario ♥ Olimpia children's book, p. 66

The relationship between compliance and autonomy is difficult to define. And perhaps it shouldn't be specified completely. There seems to be a link between friendship and admiration. Where the force of the design is overwhelming, or the personal contact is so powerful that the designers can no longer see beyond it, the focus shifts to their contribution. That was how Thonik unravelled Dick Bruna's classic children's book Boris en de paraplu in 2001. Using the original drawings, their Boris en de paraplu schetsboek reconstructed the painfully precise visual editing that Bruna employed to arrive at his minimalist illustrations.

In many ways, a recognisable Thonik product. Not least because the designers suggested the book themselves, and this being the first time that the illustrations in this work, which has sold worldwide in astronomical numbers, have been analysed like this. The original book is included in The Sketchbook as a ready-made product, but first it is compared to the pencil sketches in Bruna's archive. Experiments, abandoned story lines and the ample evidence of the author's search for the simplest, most effective way to illustrate the narrative. As Thonik attempted to demonstrate the creative process by presenting Bruna's sketches in the form of transparent overlays above the definitive drawings, their respect for the mastery that this comparison revealed grew.

Roy Villevoye, No problem, brother!

Boris en de paraplu schetsboek

The Best Book Designs poster

The ministry of education, culture and science's Cultuurnota, p. 151

De Zingende Zaag, all inside pages of issue no. 24/25 on the studio wall

The Sketchbook is by definition subservient, the focus being on Bruna's genius. Here Thonik's signature is limited to their competent categorisation and reconstruction. It reveals something of their method that they required only a few weeks to devise the concept, edit the illustrations and text, design the book and have it printed. Unlike most Thonik books, Boris en de paraplu schetsboek makes no feign moves. It's more like a forty-yard pass, chipped ingeniously over the keeper's head by Bruna. The public remember the goal; only the afficionados can recall every detail of the preceding seconds – how the ball streaked into the six-yard box at precisely the right angle.

The conceptual quality became noticeable when Thomas Widdershoven made the catalogue of the previous year's fifty Best Book Designs (De Best Verzorgde Boeken) in 1993. He took photos of all the winning designers, each holding a copy of their book. He also collected original film of the various publications, had these printed afresh and added them to his own book. Some formats were too large and had to be truncated, other were too small and were placed against a white background. These were an interpretation, literally showing the maker's hand (not his head); the printed pages reproduced the original work as neutrally as possible. In fact there's a direct line leading from The Best Book Designs (De Best Verzorgde Boeken) to Guide to Nature, artist Cor Dera's catalogue (2000) that were both nominated for the Rotterdam Design Prize (1994, 2001).
Here too, Thonik have quoted directly from existing material by cutting a nature book out of its cover and rebinding it with an added introductory section and a conclusion. The concept echoes the intentions and method of the artist but makes no attempt to present his work.
For many of their clients Gonnissen and Widdershoven had long enjoyed a recognisable signature. Discussions about a new book, periodical or house style were always an analytical process. Their questions focused on the real motives, and their suggestions often had a deceptive subtlety.
Over the years Thonik have had a constant turnover of seemingly unrelated assignments. And yet the hands that held the best designed books, reappear in the ministry of education, culture and science's Cultuurnota (2000), applauding as the reader flits through the pages.
Since 1992, Thomas Widdershoven has produced the layout for poetry magazine De Zingende Zaag, an ongoing ode to experimentation. No one issue resembles any other. Although some ideas are so serviceable that they may find a place in a different context. The trash campaign for Amsterdam's refuse department would never have been possible without the experiments in De Zingende Zaag. Poetry and trash linked like Siamese twins. That's Thonik.

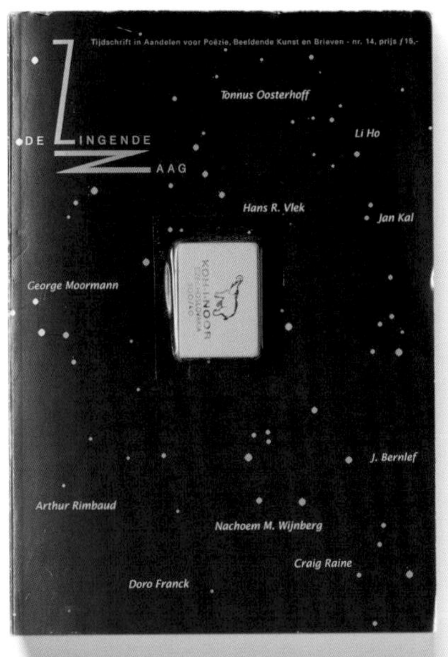
DE ZINGENDE ZAAG
Tonnus Oosterhoff
Li Ho
Hans R. Vlek
Jan Kal
George Moormann
J. Bernlef
Arthur Rimbaud
Nachoem M. Wijnberg
Craig Raine
Doro Franck

DE ZINGENDE ZAAG
O
K
knock-out
by poetry

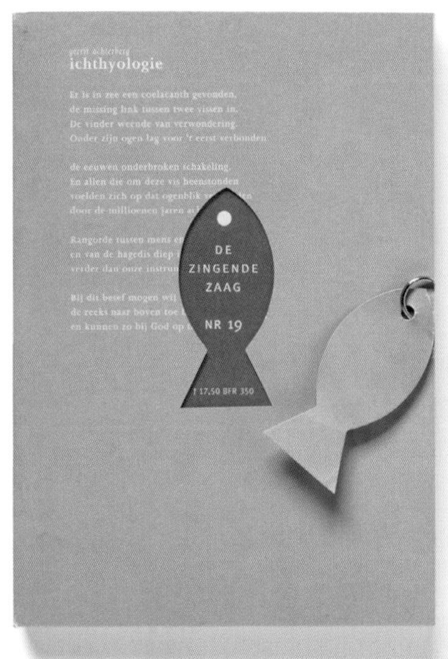
ichthyologie
DE ZINGENDE ZAAG
NR 19

De Zingende Zaag nr.24/25
manifesten van de jaren negentig
DE ZINGENDE ZAAG
ja
het koekoeksnest

ZIG ZAG
de zingende zaag 21 en 22
poëzie als kinderspel

de tas van
Rodenko

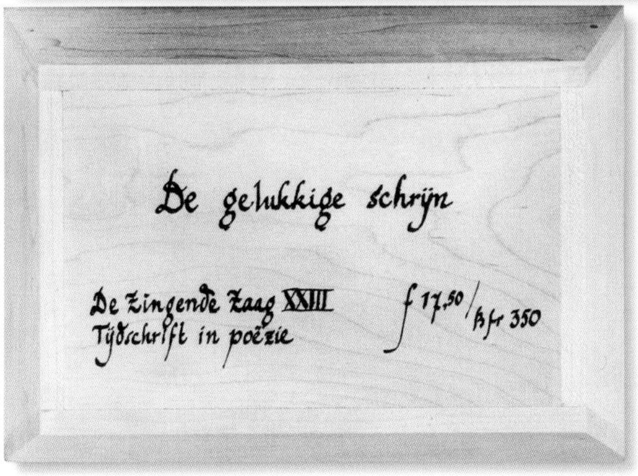

onthulling

centraal
museum

wereldwijd
worldwide

cmclub

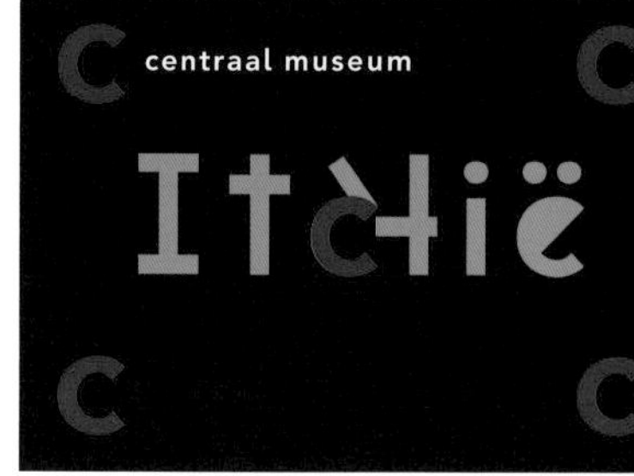

rietveld
schröderhuis

00.00

Open van wo t/m zon

Prins Hendriklaan 50
3583 EP Utrecht
T +31 (0)30 236 23 10
F +31 (0)30 233 20 06

rietveld
schröderhuis

Open van wo t/m zon

Prins Hendriklaan 50
3583 EP Utrecht
T +31 (0)30 236 23 10
F +31 (0)30 233 20 06

www.panorama2000.com

PANORAMA
2000

centraal
museum

vrije
ceramiek

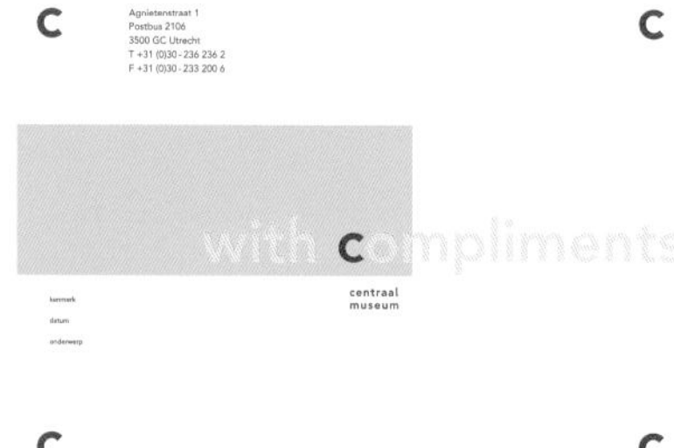

kids
centraal

centraal
museum

www.centraalmuseum.nl

centraal museum krant

Open, open!! | Panorama 2000 | Ronald Giphart | GRATIS

made in japan

r u o t e

fiets en wandel

c-style

abcdefg

hijklmn

opqrstu

vwxyz?!

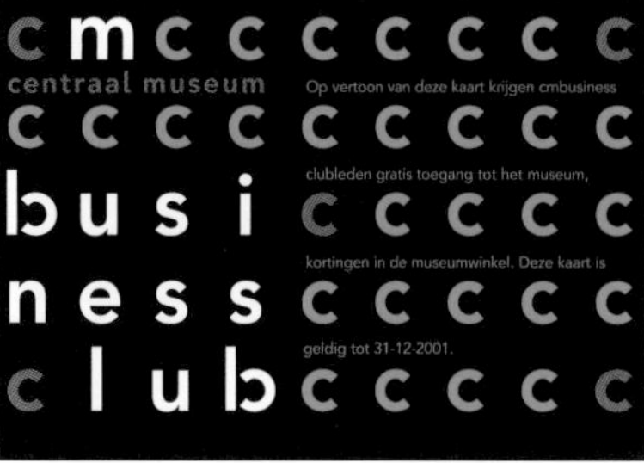

centraal museum

carsten höller

geluk

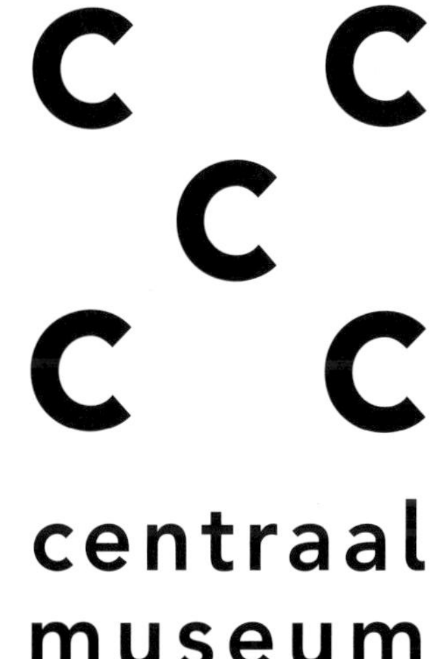

persbericht
persbericht
persbericht
centraal museum

centraal museum krant

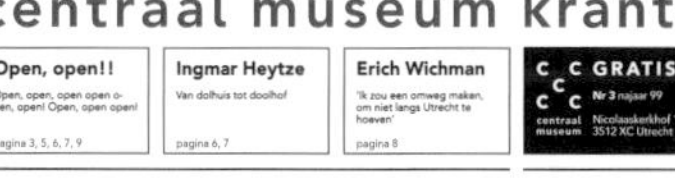

OPEN

OPEN

OPEN

Open, open open open open, open!

cmclub

centraal museum

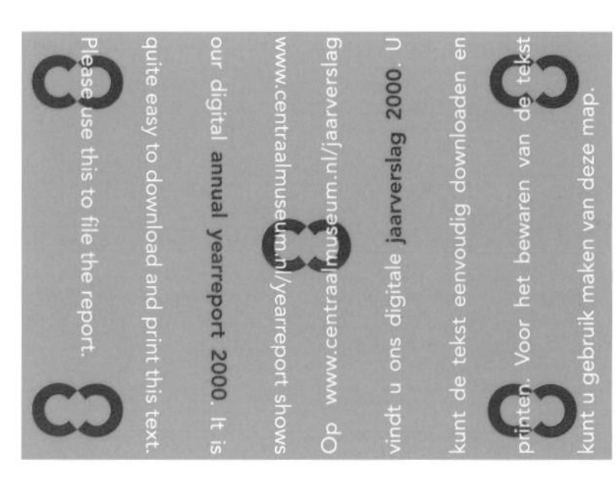

Najaar 2000

C-01

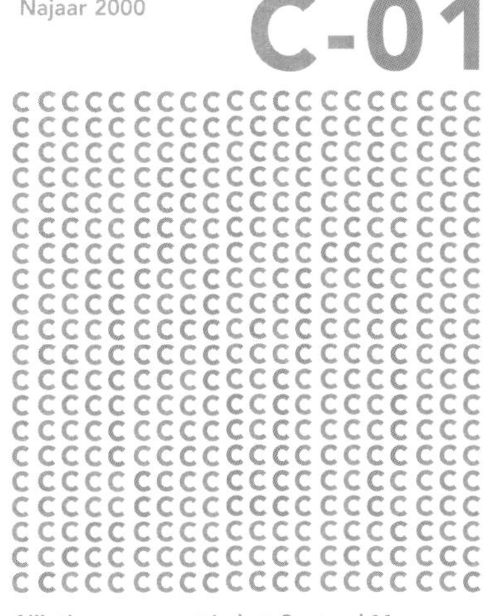

Nijntje permanent in het Centraal Museum

Saenredam Relatiearrangement

centraal museum krant

Licht | Familie | Solo | GRATIS

caravaggisten

meesters van het licht

PANORAMA
2000

2000

PANORAMA

c c
c
c c

centraal
museum

2000

PANORAMA

c c
c
c c

centraal
museum

2000

PANORAMA

c c
c
c c

centraal
museum

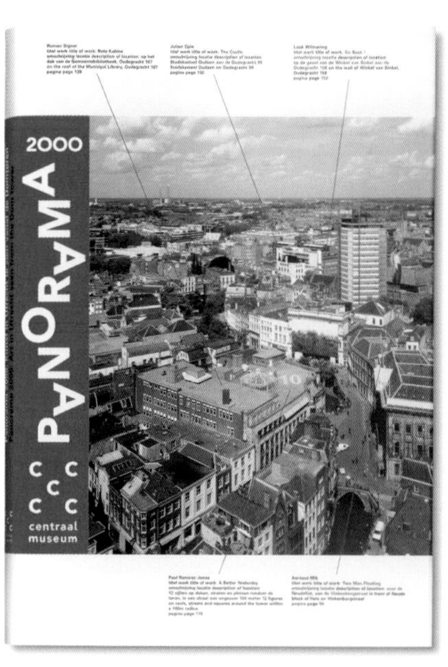
2000
PANORAMA
centraal
museum

centraal museum krant

Open, open!!

Open, open, open open o-pen, open! Open, open open!

pagina 3, 5, 6, 7, 9

Ingmar Heytze

Van dolhuis tot doolhof

pagina 6, 7

Erich Wichman

'Ik zou een omweg maken, om niet langs Utrecht te hoeven'

pagina 8

GRATIS

Nr 3 najaar 99

centraal museum

Nicolaaskerkhof 10
3512 XC Utrecht

Open, open open open open, open!

Open, open open! Open! Open! open, open, open! Open open, o-pen open! Open! open! Open o-pen open open, open! Open! open open! Open!!!
Open open open open. Open, open. Open open Open! Open! Open. Open, open, o-pen! Open open open open! Open, open! Open! Open! open, open, open open.

Open! Open! open, open, open open. Open! Open, open open! Open! Open! open, open, open! Open open, open.O-pen! Open open open open, open! Open! open! Open!
Open! Open, open, open. Open open open open! Open, open! Open open o-pen open! Open, open! Open open, open! Open! Open open open open, open! O-pen. Open! Open! Open, open, open! O-pen. Open. Open, open, open!

Open! Open! Open!

Open! open! open, open! Open. Open open open, open! open, open! Open! O-pen open! open! open! Open, open, open! Open open open open! Open, open! open! Open! Open! open, open, open open o-pen! Open, open open. Open! Open! open, Open open open open! Open, open! Open! Open! Open! open, open, open open.Open, open open! Open. Open! open, open! Open open open open! Open, open! Open!!!
Open! Open! open, open, open open. O-pen! Open, open open! Open. Open! open open, open! Open open,open!

OPEN

c-style

abcdef

ghijklm

nopqrs

tuvwxy

z?!

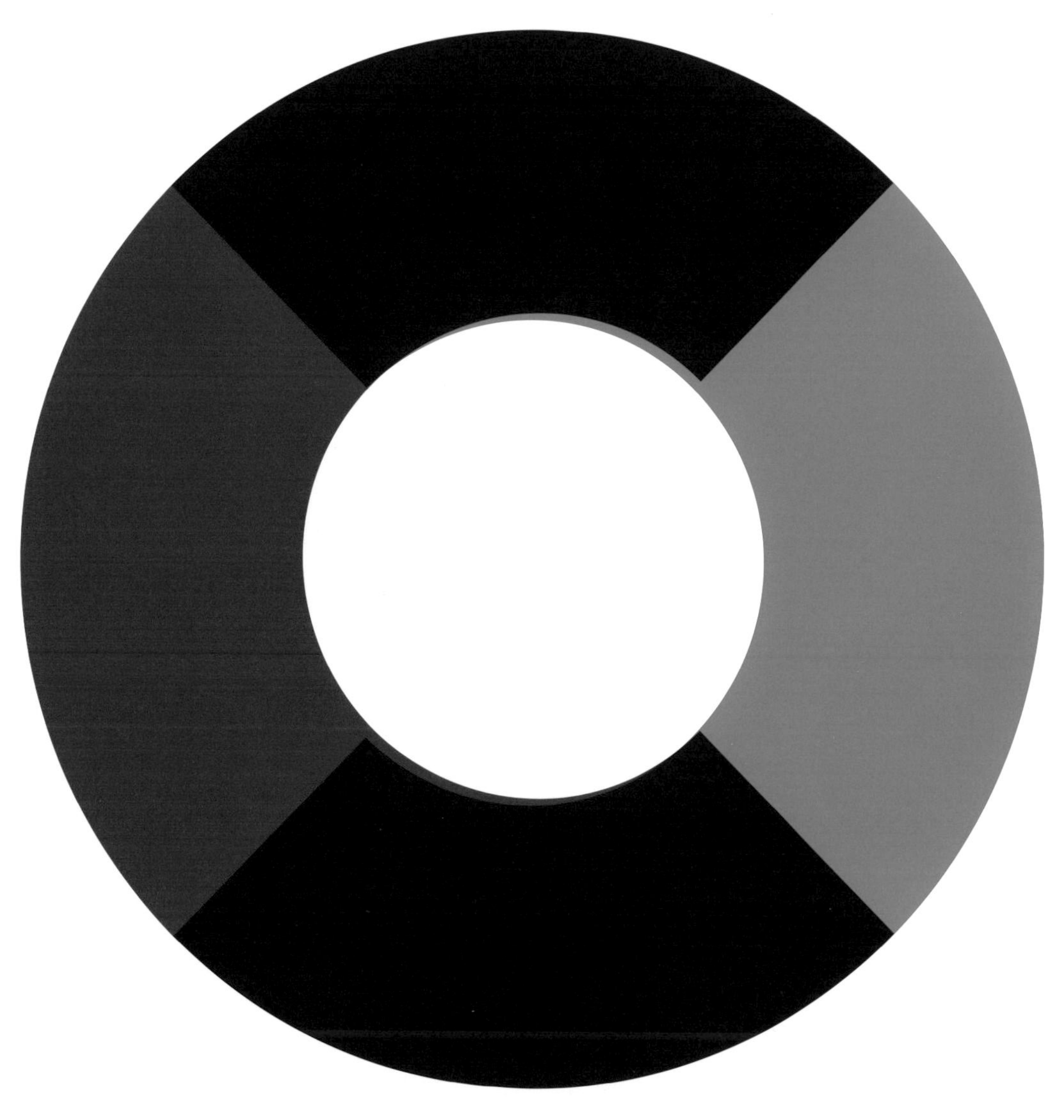

kids
centraal

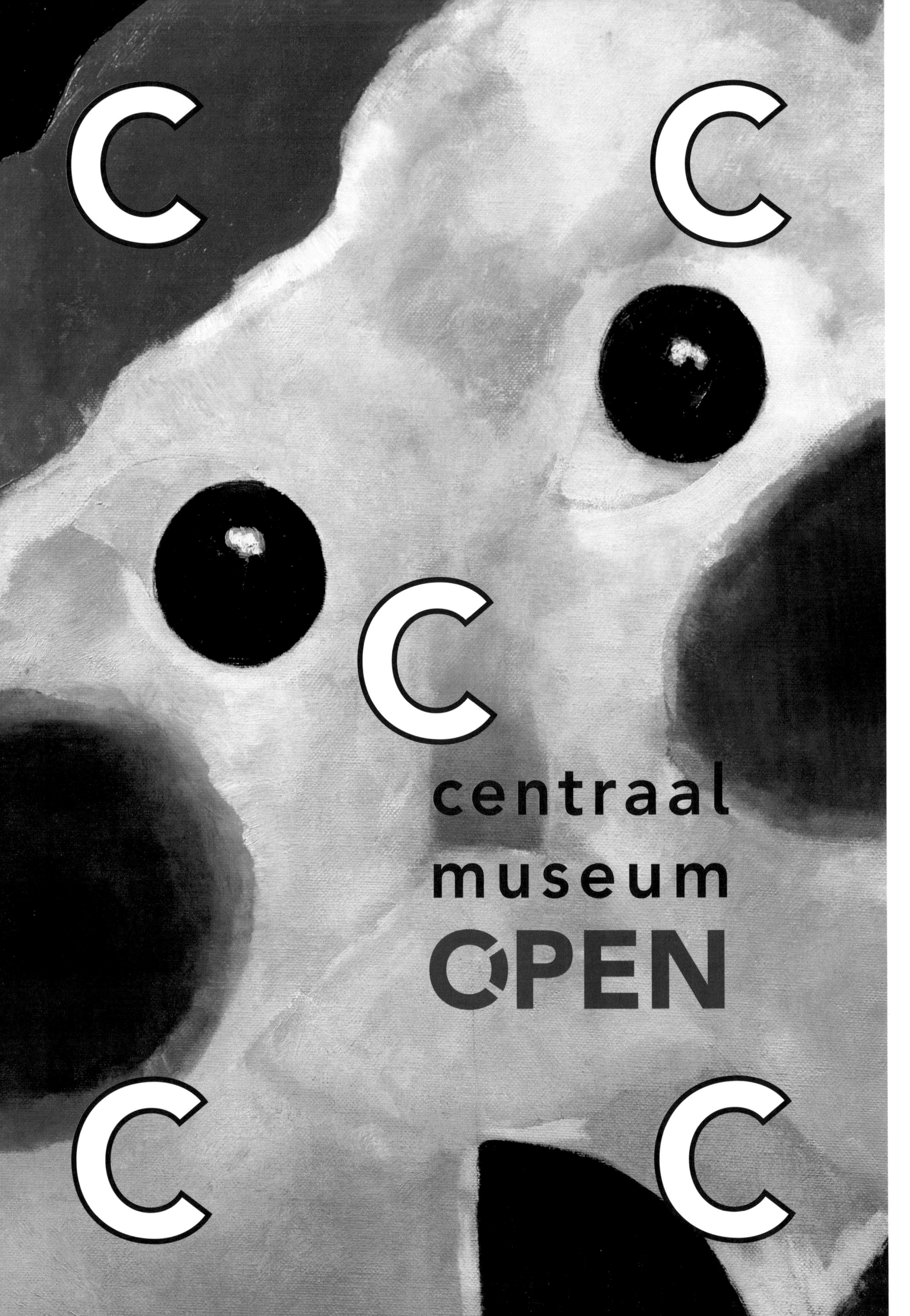
centraal
museum
OPEN

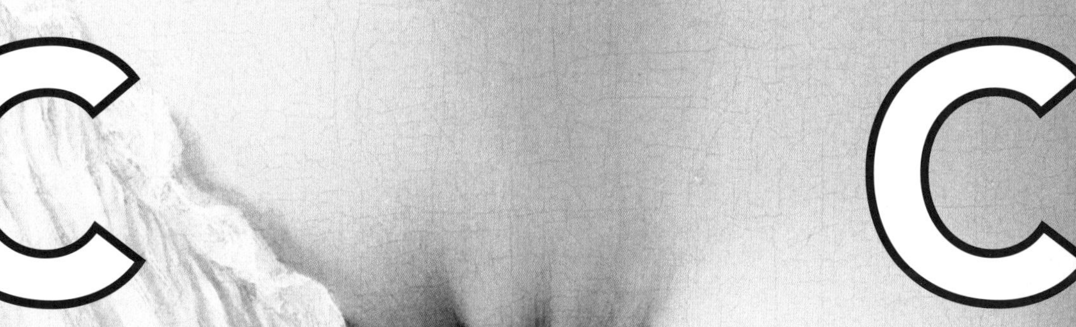
centraal
museum
OPEN

Scorel
centraal museum

centraal museum

wereldwijd
worldwide

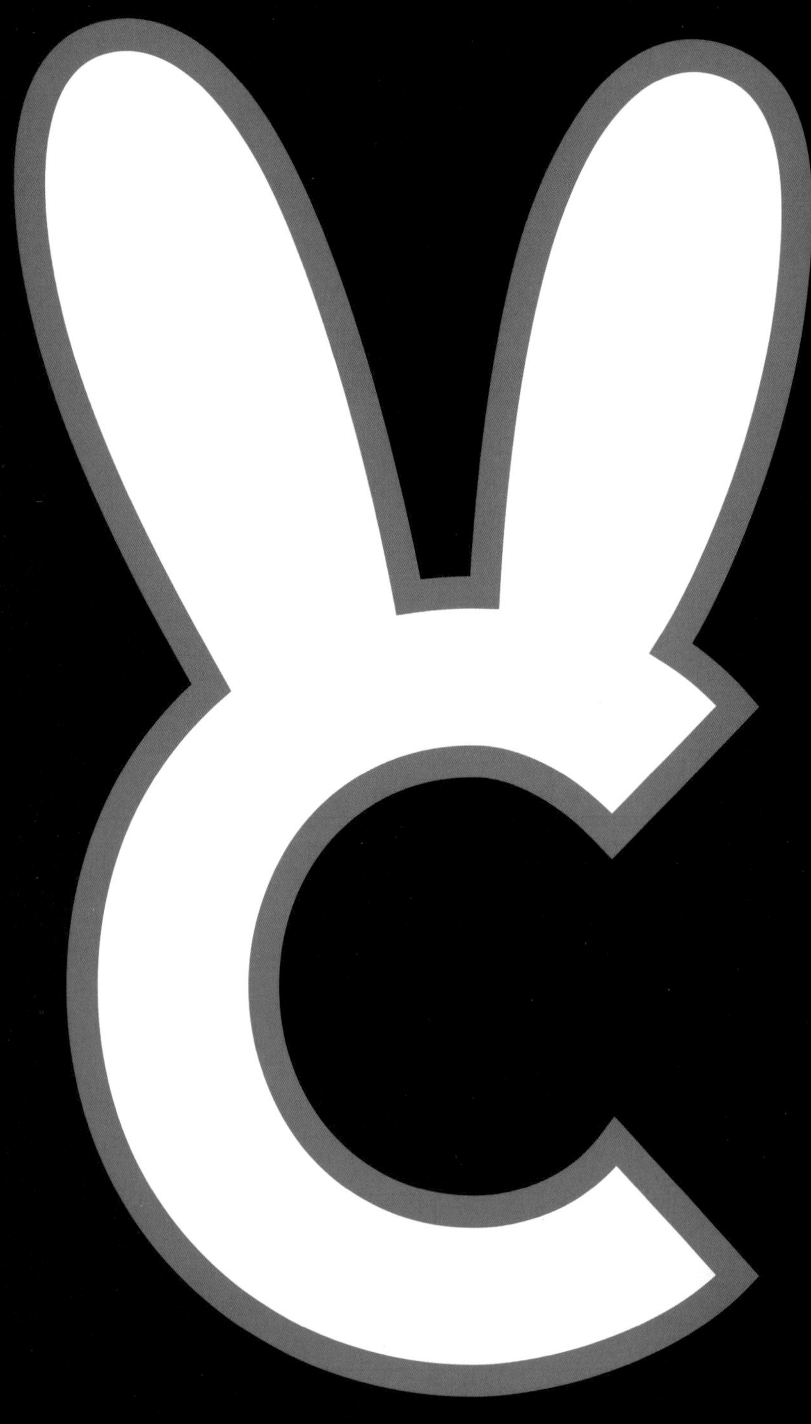

dick bruna

www.centraalmuseum.nl
O
P
centraal
museum
vanaf 28-11-1999
EN
c c
c
c c
centraal
museum

documenta

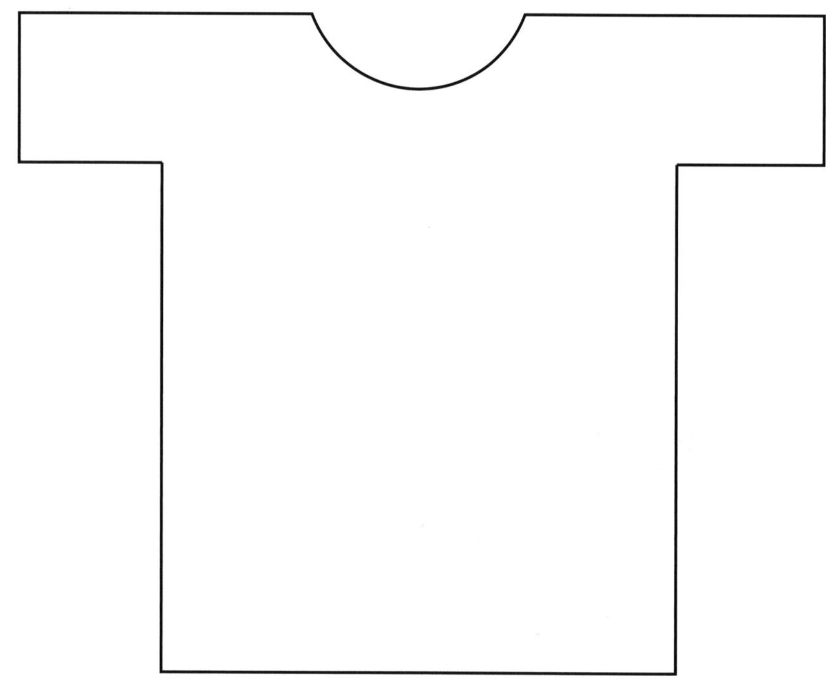

FRICTION
SISTA

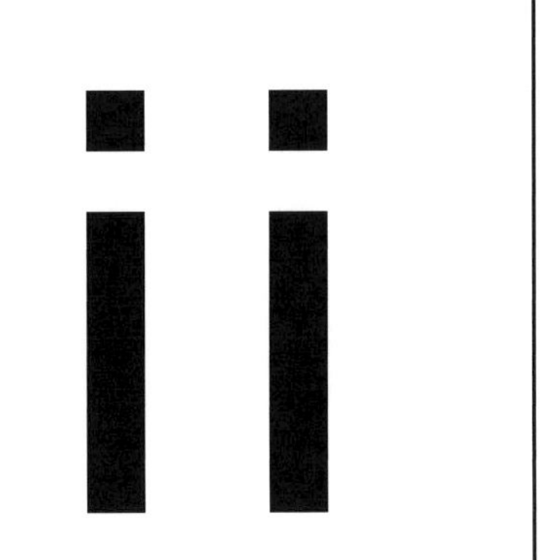

2002 roman numerals for two	eleven	i for inter inter-disciplininary interaction international
two people	i and i two individuals meeting	a face two eyes two i's

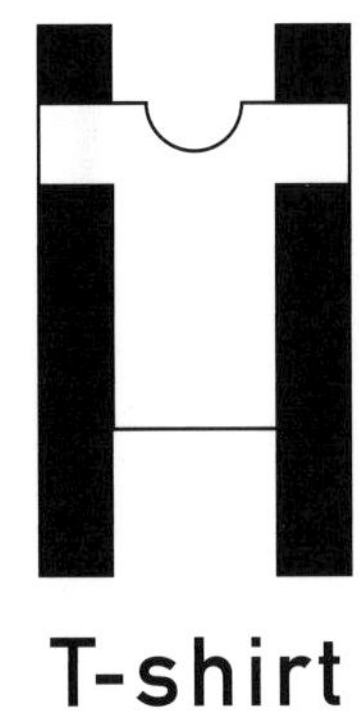

T-shirt

burada

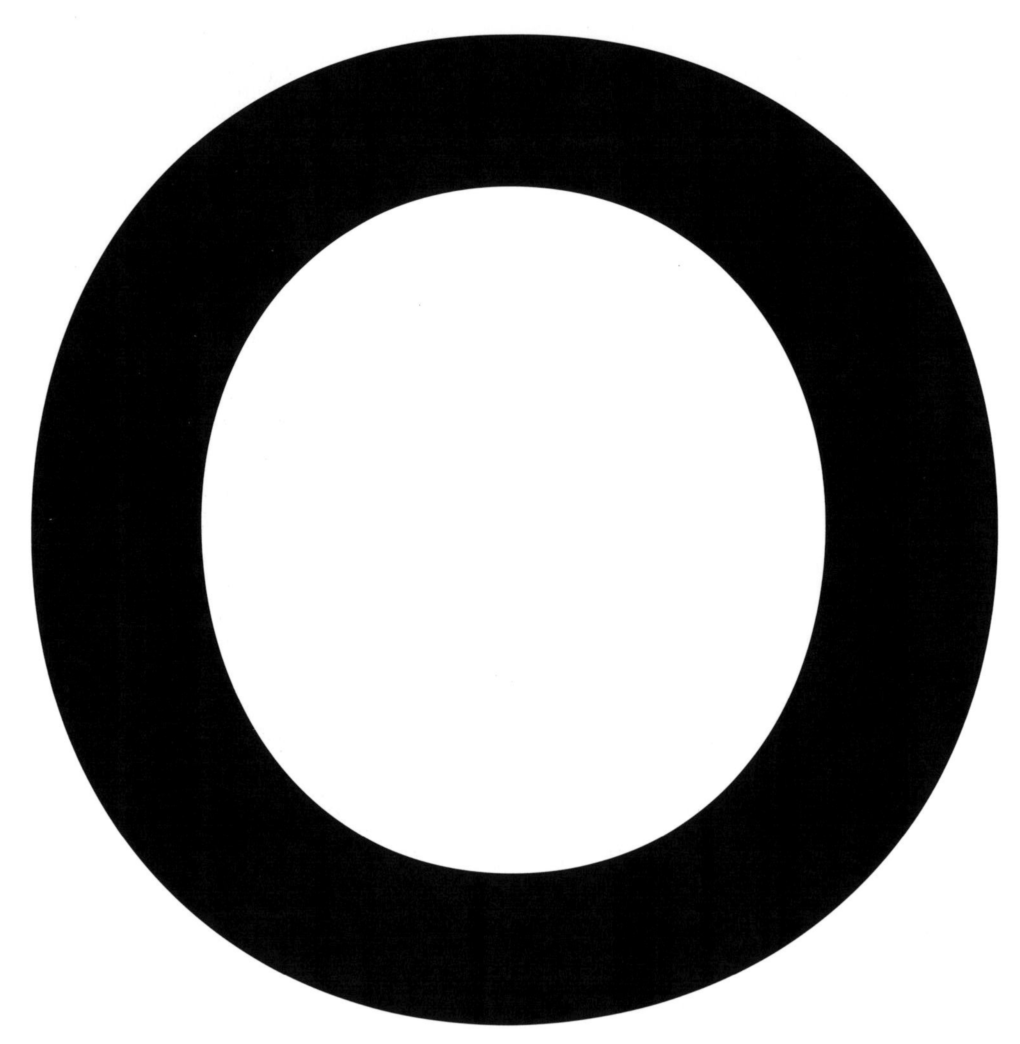

SOX

SUX

H E T V E R L A
N G E N N A A R
A R C H I T E C
T U U R E N D E
B E S L O M M E
R I N G E N V A
N A L L E D A G

WIEL ARETS WIM VAN DEN BERGH RALPH BRODRÜCK MATTHIEU BRULS JO COENEN BERT DIRRIX TOM FRANTZEN BABET GALIS PASCAL GROSFELD MARTIEN JANSEN ERIK KNIPPERS BART LOOTSMA ANNETTE MARX & ADY STEKETEE JEROEN SCHIPPER ROB SMITS SJOERD SOETERS BERT STAAL RUDY UYTENHAAK GERT JAN WILLEMSE RENÉ VAN ZUUK REDACTIE BART LOOTSMA EN MARIËTTE VAN STRALEN UITGEVERIJ THOTH BUSSUM

HETVERLANGENNAARARCHITECTUUR ENDEBESLOMMERINGENVANALLEDAG THOTH

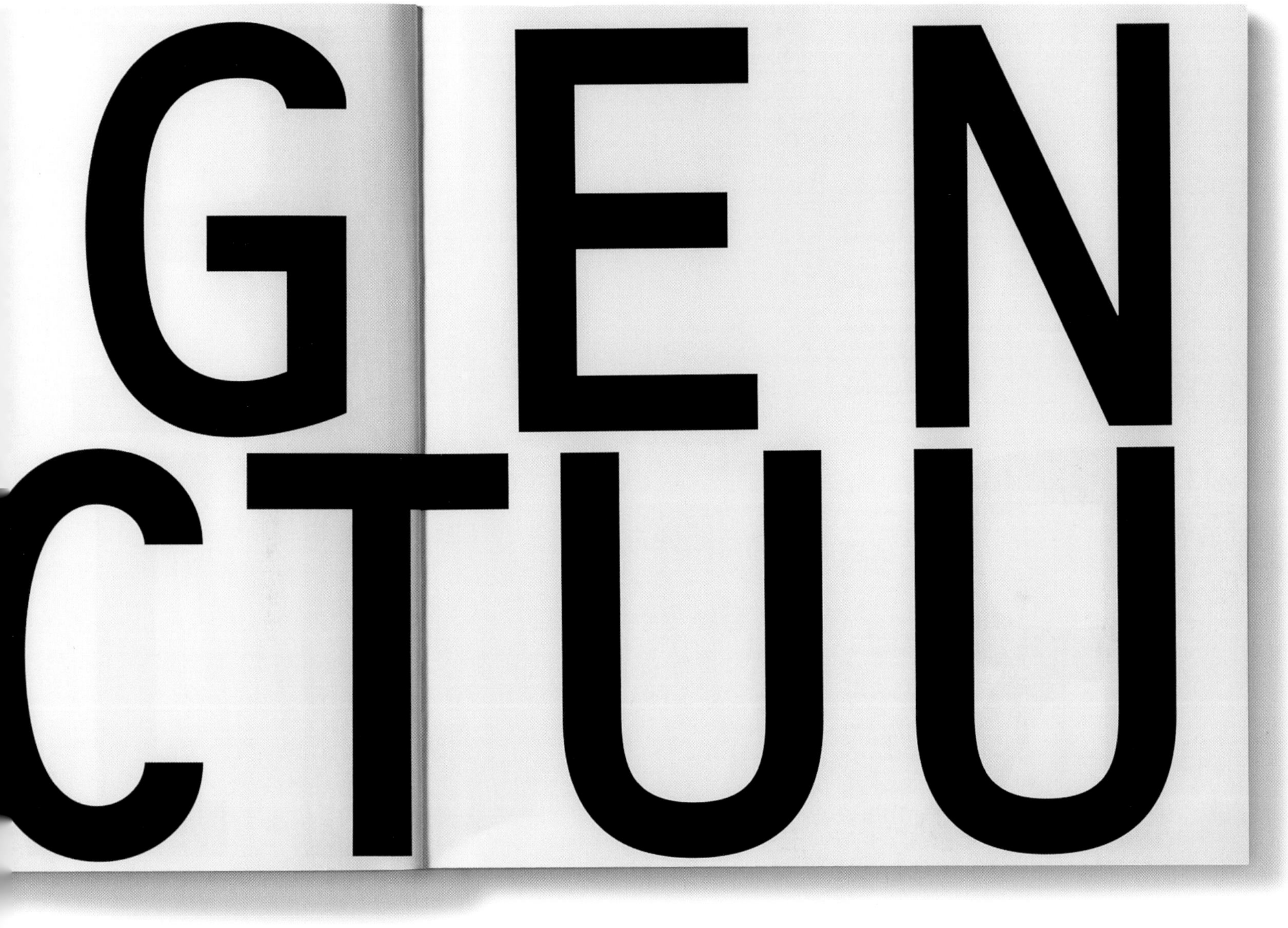

GEN
CTUU

ACE

VERLAN

E
N

1 APR - 30 JUN 2000

OVER
THE E
DGES

GENT

Keizer Karel 1500-2000. Een rijk waar de zon niet ondergaat

1-4 / 30-6 GENT GAND
OVER
THE E
DGES
GENT
ST-LIEVENSPOORT

1 APR - 30 JUN 2000

E

GE

NT

Keizer Karel 1500-2000. Een rijk waar de zon niet ondergaat

1-4 / 30-6 GENT GAND
E
E
DGES
S.M.A.K.

1 APR - 30 JUN 2000

E

E E

E

E

Keizer Karel 1500-2000. Een rijk waar de zon niet ondergaat

My SecondSkin
SCHIESSER
E
E
E
OVER
THE E
DGES
GENT

DROOG DESIGN 1
NARCISSE TOR
HARRY
RUHÉ
WIM T. SCHI

eternally yours
visions on product endurance
1-1996
centraal museum
centraal museum
PERS
centraal museum

HETHE BESTE VANOF WIM T. SCHIPPERS

HARRY RUHÉ

er eleven
Hoofdstuk

ch the television adventures of a night-club owner
ebated, and The Onan sinks ingloriously

n de televisieavonturen van een nachtclubeigenaar en behandeld, en De Onan roemloos ten onder gaat

lière van Nederland. Dát was Wim T. Schippers volgens Gied s. In een interview met de Haagse Post legde hij uit waarom: 'Ik emand die zulke ad remme dialogen kan schrijven. (...) Molière. In men van grootte denk ik. Als Wim iets maakt, kun je nooit zeggen geïnspireerd is door een ander. Dat is zeer ongebruikelijk.'[1] ding voor het vraaggesprek was de presentatie van *Elly* in Carré. et script van die produktie zei Jaspars: 'Wim is een echte perfec- Je zult geen enkel script in heel Nederland vinden met zo'n aan- voor het minutieuze detail. Dat is Wim. Ook dat-ie in dat detail- oms de grote lijnen wel eens uit het oog verliest. Ik heb daar varing mee.' jaren geleden werd Schippers geïnterviewd in het Amsterdamse ik. Tijdens het bestijgen van de befaamde marmeren trap noteert nalist de volgende regels: "'Wat?!' Hij wijst op een van de beu- aarmee de trapleuning aan de muur is bevestigd. 'Hier horen vier fjes in te zitten, maar het zijn er maar drie.'"[2] Toen kort geleden teartikel ter sprake kwam, zei Schippers: 'Als ik in het museum ik altijd even kijken. Wist je dat ze er nog steeds niets aan gedaan?' s: 'Wim kan zich diepe zorgen maken over de klink van een deur, de rest van het huis in brand staat.' die 'aandacht voor het minutieuze detail' van wezenlijk belang. s al zo geweest bij zijn beeldende werk uit de jaren zestig - de it van een werk als *Luxuria* (1965) wordt voor een belangrijk deel d door de fraaie detaillering en de uiterst zorgvuldige afwerking onderdelen - en in Schippers' omgang met de taal is dat niet . Van acteurs die zijn teksten voordragen, verwacht hij dan ook zich nauwgezet aan het script houden. Ook (of beter: juist) als ingewikkelde of ongebruikelijke zinsconstructies gaat. Bekend erhaal dat Harry Touw in zijn rol van Fred Haché mensen uit- voor 'gehaktbal' telkens als er in het script stond: 'bal gehakt'. zenlijk verschil.

Al in het vroegste werk Assemblages heten *Ho* ningen krijgen titels 'm *zilveren pet* (1962). In teksten gecombineerd jaren lang wordt er gev een boek 'vol vervelen *for Advanced Studies* tiek van de eigentijdse Verenigde Staten') en pelijke werkjes' om zic Ook in de shows rond een belangrijke rol. Va voor, inclusief het verk gen die daar soms bijh het wel lukt eventueel dig gesleuteld: ('De tee gevallen lijken de teks ('Oppassen Barend, ee doende woordconstru ('De Duivel zal een jeg voor dat Nederlandse, door elkaar worden ge de Koningin op bezoek Allons! Courage. Polle dicht. Op hoop van zeg Dit ongebruikelijke taa Veel van de woorden *a* gedurende korte of lan woord gekte, dat al in e En verder: *Prima de lu* *nerveu* (Servet). Ook w de uitdrukking *Ik word* populair. Overigens is niet allee boodschap zelf vaak w de trein in België zijn a hoe 'n mooie omgevin zie je in Nederland toc *Het is weer zo laat*, me Waldo van Dungen, ko voor. Wanneer Waldo's schappen doen plotse leven is na de dood?', 'Nou mevrouwtje, ik de het nog zal meemaken

HARRY RUHÉ
WIM T. SCHIPPERS
BILINGUAL EDITION
TWEETALIGE EDITIE
centraal museum

u

ve
fdstuk

ention is made of a Moving Floor, an Indian
hristmas tree and Twenty-five Identical Clocks

ake is van een Bewegende Vloer, een
erstboom en Vijfentwintig Identieke Klokken

e spot gedreven met de heiligste gevoelens van een le are
n het Nederlandse Volk. Wordt het geen tijd dat de minis-
en komt? Anders moeten de kerken er maar iets aan gaan
were spoken by the Reverend L.L. Blok and were
e regels zijn van dominee L.L. Blok. Ze werden in het
69 afgedrukt in het krantje 'Hervormd Amsterdam'. sive
aal niet om een kwetsend tv-programma, maar om een
en tijdelijk kunstwerk van Wim T. Schippers.
1969 verrees aan het Amsterdamse Leidseplein, vlak alls
in, een groot formaat kerstboom, fraai opgetuigd met of
allen. Er was een grijze vlag naast gezet, maar die viel
o. Eigenlijk was het de bedoeling dat de naaldboom onifer
zomer zou worden geïnstalleerd, maar dat werd als wer-
tst beschouwd; september kon nog nét. 'In fantasieloos
Den Haag zou zo'n voorstel natuurlijk terstond van de
ezen. Zo echter niet in het pulserend, swingend
nopperde Het Vrije Volk. aper Het Vrije Volk.
r was het Rembrandtsplein aan de beurt. In het zomerse
vijfentwintig identieke stadsklokken neergezet, die ook e
fde tijd aangaven. Verder werd het plein opgesierd met
lichtbakken die de richting aangaven naar onder meer
'Bugpeh', 'Knetten', 'Driehelb' en 'AvPlu'. Sommige
en het wel aardig, maar bij anderen veroorzaakte het pro-
g en woede. Zo werd er veel geklaagd over de zinloos-
e lijken wel gek bij de gemeente' - en het vele 'verspilde'
e gemoeid zou zijn. Dat laatste viel overigens wel mee,
ewerkt met bestaand materiaal en na afloop, eind sep-
de klokken weer op andere plaatsen te gebruiken.

kunst wel wat kosten, maar dan moet het er ook als run
. In elk plantsoen staat wel een beeld. Ook in het rt.
water drijft veel kunst. Artistiek vormgegeven 'lichtlij-

nen' in het plaveisel, sculpturale lantaarnpalen... zo erg als nu was het
in 1969 nog niet, maar ook toen al was Amsterdam de stad met de it is
grootste kunstdichtheid van Nederland. e city with the greatest
Een enkele keer wordt er eens wat gemopperd. Dan is een tussen
huizen opgeworpen kunstwerk van dusdanige afmetingen dat omlig-
gende bewoners het uitzicht wordt ontnomen. Of dan wordt een uit
metalen platen opgebouwd beeld door nachtelijke dronkelappen stel-
selmatig als percussie-instrument gebruikt. Maar over het algemeen
wordt er veel geaccepteerd. Ooit stond er in de buurt ighbourhood
een fraaie 'antieke' zonnewijzer. Het vorige 'antique' sun dial. It
gerekte strook groen to an elongated strip of shrubbery along a
was het Amsterdam avenue. One day the elegant instrument
suddenly disappeared to make way for a concrete block, ten metres
high. There was definitely art afoot. The neighbours resigned
themselves to the new situation. Apparently 'art' has something to
do with living in the big city just like stench, noise pollution and
pigeon droppings. And you get used to it after a while.
On the other hand, the works that Schippers erected in the city
were usually temporary; after a few weeks or months they were
dismantled leaving the site in its original state. So too sculptures
specially made for exhibitions were sometimes destroyed
afterwards, like the Vondelpark *Sofa* and the contribution towards
Sonsbeek 71 (For the event *Sonsbeek buiten de perken*, (Sonsbeek
beyond bounds), Schippers created a car made of reinforced
sandstone, spray-painted in a sandstone-like colour, that had lost
had nul and 'skidded' against a (real) tree: 'I felt like erecting an
keer zessive sculpture for a change. This car is twice life size. It's a
Rivièra between a Buick-Rivièra and an old Chrysler, with a modern
ouderwd an old-fashioned rear. A bit like a car in a colouring
Ik dwaal
baasd drifting from the subject. What I mean to say is that it
dan een ed me at the time that an *Indian Summer Christmas tree*
de omwouse more commotion than a ten metre high sculptural
Overigen block, which moreover, remains a permanent burden for
zorgen. Dunding tenants. However Schippers always managed to
voorzien little extra confusion. The self-effacing manner with which
die plek') ed to every new 'cultural provision' ('rather an old idea',
iemand de might look nice over there') did not exactly help in
kunstenaar understanding. When, on one occasion someone
commented 'surely that's not art', the artist replied, 'You never
heard me say it was'.
Al in 1965 ha
aangekondig 965 Schippers had announced that he planned
worden voor the foodstuffs branch'. At Steendrukkerij de Jong &
produkten op had to be covered with a thin layer of peanut butter.
'Ik heb ook eets, like lemonade tasting of fish, were also to be

Mario ♥ Olimpia
Mario ♥ Olimpia

De *aartseng*
men, gewap
schild en bl
rechters-flu
De duivels
allen een m
Een groots
Carnaval!

ıt aanstor-
et zwaard en
zijn scheids-

n met z'n
lucht in.
kel.

Het giebelen verandert in zingen. De meisjes-stemmen zingen een lied uit Mario's geboorte-streek. Uit het lied stijgt opeens een stem op, zo mooi, zo hoog, niet van deze wereld. Als de *Maagd* zou zingen, moet het zó klinken, wonderschoon, een hemelse stem. Mario krijgt tranen in zijn ogen.
Hij blijft als betoverd staan. De kerkdeuren zwaaien open. Het beeldje van de Maagd wordt naar buiten gedragen in een dichte stroom van mensen.

Dit is het jaarverslag van het Wereld Natuur Fonds

Dit is het jaarverslag van het Wereld Natuur Fonds

Een leefbare wereld met een rijke natuur achterlaten voor de kinderen van vandaag; dat is het doel van het Wereld Natuur Fonds. En hoewel het óns doel is, weten we zeker dat wij dat niet alleen kunnen realiseren. Daarom hebben we anderen nodig. Die anderen kunnen ondernemers zijn, politici, consumenten, werknemers, kinderen. Kortom, iedereen die bereid is dagelijks handelen zo vorm te geven dat de natuur en het milieu daar beter van worden.

Wij zoeken helpende handen. Die handen kunnen een cheque aanreiken (dat moet zelfs, want zonder geld beginnen we al helemaal niets), maar ze kunnen ook heel concreet energiebesparende maatregelen nemen, of alleen duurzaam geproduceerd hout gebruiken. Thuis, maar ook in uw bedrijf.

Wij zoeken u! Hoe en waar leest u in dit beknopte jaarverslag. Met opzet beknopt, omdat we graag willen en hopen dat u het ook daadwerkelijk leest.

En laat vooropgezet zijn: wij zijn realisten, we gaan economische ontwikkelingen niet met een botaniseertrommeltje te lijf. Wij denken alleen dat veel zaken anders en beter kunnen. Nee, móeten. Wanneer u enkele minuten de tijd hebt, vertellen we in 't kort hoe.

Ed Nijpels
voorzitter

Siegfried Woldhek
directeur

NB. De achterzijde van dit jaarverslag mag u pas bekijken nadat u de inhoud in zijn geheel gelezen heeft!

WWF

Wat doet een bever De bever bouwt langs de waterkant aan de natuur. Zelfs de dikste bomen knaagt hij door. Op zoek naar takken om een burcht mee te bouwen. Op zoek naar jonge scheuten die tot zijn voedselpakket behoren. Waar de bever bomen heeft geveld, ontstaan open plekken in het bos. Dat levert variatie in de vegetatie op en daar krijgen insekten, vogels en zoogdieren een kans. Bevers trekken ook rond. Als ze zich vanuit de Gelderse Poort gaan verspreiden, kan de bever zich langs Waal, Nederrijn, IJssel en Maas vestigen. Ze kunnen ook het contact tussen Biesbosch en de Duitse bevergebieden langs Hase en Rur tot stand brengen.

Beverpartners Op 30 september 1994 zijn twaalf bevers uitgezet. Drie maanden later zijn er vier overleden, drie door de ziekte van Weil, een door ouderdom. Moeilijk, maar zo gaat dat bij herintroductie. Bij een ander, uiteindelijk succesvol project, stierf in het begin maar liefst 95% van de dieren. Dus hebben we goede hoop, want de overgebleven dieren doen het goed. Nieuwe natuur bouw je samen met partners op. In de werkgroep *Bevers in de Gelderse Poort* zitten - behalve het WNF - Staatsbosbeheer, de provincie Gelderland, het ministerie van Landbouw, Natuurbeheer en Visserij, en het onderzoeksinstituut IBN/DLO.

Wat kost één bever?

Zo'n tweeduizend gulden. Niet zo heel veel dus. En het is ook niet helemaal waar. De natuur is eigenlijk onbetaalbaar. En gelukkig dat je uit het buitenland nog bevers kunt halen. Die tweeduizend gulden zijn puur de kosten van het vangen in Duitsland, het transport naar Nederland en het uitzetten in de Millingerwaard. Maar daarmee waren we er natuurlijk nog niet. De bevers worden met een onderzoeksprogramma gevolgd. En uiteraard hebben we dit project met heel veel publiciteit begeleid. Want zo'n kans krijg je niet elke dag. Video's, folders, een tentoonstelling, een informatieavond voor de bewoners uit de omgeving en het bezoek van vele journalisten. Allemaal investeringen in de toekomst. En waarom? Omdat de bever een kleine maar ó zo belangrijke schakel is in de Gelderse Poort. Omdat hij ruimte maakt, door takken en bomen weg te halen.

f 1,82

Omdat hij met zijn dammen de waterloop beïnvloedt. Omdat je daarmee variatie in de begroeiing krijgt. Omdat daarmee het gebied in beweging blijft. Dat maakt het weer aantrekkelijk voor andere dieren, en voor planten die verdwenen waren maar nu weer terugkomen. Dan keert de stern steeds terug. En misschien zelfs de zeearend. Daarmee wordt natuur weer natuur. En dát is weer belangrijk voor iedereen. Zo'n klein beestje, met zo'n grote invloed.

Hoe kunt u helpen?

Een kleine schakel kan een hele keten herstellen. Alle beetjes helpen. Milieuzorg in het eigen bedrijf levert winst op, hoe dan ook. Misschien is het wel mogelijk om - in overleg met anderen - binnen de eigen bedrijfsvoering de natuur een rol te laten spelen. Hier wordt nog steeds enigszins lacherig over gesproken. Maar wat zegt ir F. Gietema, directeur van de Grontmij, op 1 december 1994 tijdens het partnersymposium van WNF en Grontmij: 'Als één van de grootste ingenieursburo's voeren wij tientallen projecten uit voor gemeenten, provincies, waterschappen. Vanuit ethische én economische motieven staat Grontmij pal achter de doelstelling voor 2.000 km^2 nieuwe natuur in Nederland. Natuurontwikkeling is een groeimarkt.' Of zoals Ed Nijpels het zei: 'Waar partijen met ogenschijnlijk tegenovergestelde belangen in een strategische alliantie samenwerken, is vaak voor beiden méér winst te boeken dan voor ieder apart.'

before

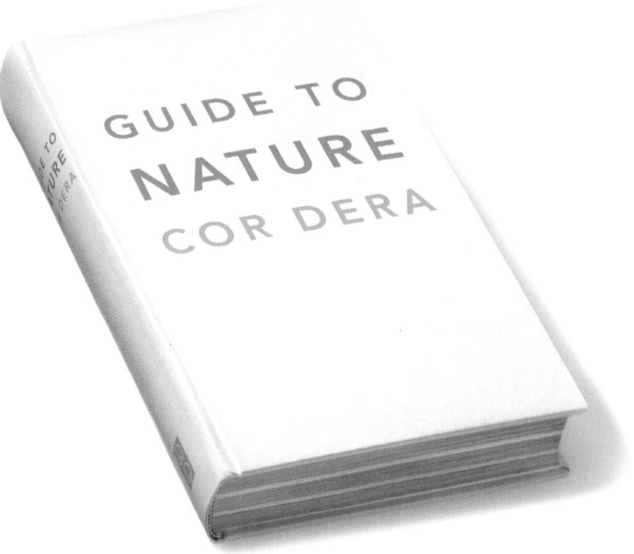

after

GUIDE TO
NATURE
COR DERA

ISBN 90-6450-279-X

9 789064 502798

Archiprix 1996
De beste studentenplannen / The Best Plans by Dutch Students
Archiprix 1996
010

DE BEST VERZORGDE BOEKEN 93
ANTON
DE KRACHT VAN HEBBEN
KPN '92/93
SONSBEEK 93
De Best Verzorgde Boeken
The Best Book Designs
93

Barnett
NOTES
Newman
24

15 Beeld tegen Beeld *Wild Plakken*

Dit is de catalogus van de gelijknamige tentoonstelling in het Centraal Museum in Utrecht. Koortsachtig, bijna wanhopig pogen de kunstenaars, de grafisch ontwerpers verenigd in het collectief 'Wild Plakken', hun engagement tot uitdrukking te brengen. Dat lukt ze beter in het werk zelf dan in de teksten die weer het materiaal voor dat werk zijn. In bonte ordening trekken meningen, affiches, schetsen en krabbels, fotomontages aan de beschouwer voorbij; alles even prachtig gedrukt. In de lay-out is de hartstocht en de chaos terug te vinden van waaruit wordt gewerkt, geplakt en gepraat. Ja, de samenleving moet veranderd en de kunstenaar heeft het moeilijk. Zo boos, zo heftig zal het wel niet meer terugkomen en daarom is het goed dat dit tegendraadse hoogtepunt van 'linkse' typografie is bekroond.

AUTEURS *authors* Max Bruinsma, Lies Ros, Rob Schröder, Pauline Terreehorst, Gerard de Vries UITGEVER *publisher* Stichting Uitgeverij De Balie, Amsterdam VERTALING *translation* Michael Gould OPLAGE *print run* 1.500 OMVANG *number of pages* 124 p. BINDWIJZE *binding style* genaaid gebrocheerd in omslag met flappen PUBLIEKSPRIJS *price* ƒ 50,- ISBN 90 6617 119 7 VORMGEVING, TYPOGRAFIE, ILLUSTRATIES EN FOTOGRAFIE *design, typography, illustrations and photography* Lies Ros, Rob Schröder (Wild Plakken) ZETWERK EN DRUK *typesetting and printing* Drukkerij R. Stolk, Amsterdam LITHOGRAFIE *lithography* Grafi-Scan vof, Amsterdam (kleur); Color Techniek, Amsterdam/Drukkerij R. Stolk, Amsterdam (z/w) DRUK OMSLAG *printing cover* Henderson Zeefdruk, Amsterdam BINDWERK *binding* Boekbinderij Verkerke bv, Alkmaar PAPIERLEVERANCIERS *paper supplies* Proost en Brandt nv, Diemen (omslag), Scaldia Papier bv, Nijmegen/GrafischPapier bv, Andelst MATERIAAL OMSLAG *material cover* hv sulfaatkarton Invercote G, 300 g/m² PAPIER BINNENWERK *paper interior* hv wit mc Twincoat silk, 150 g/m²; Pordenone naturel, 100 g/m² LETTERTYPEN *typefaces* Frutiger, Symbol BOEKFORMAAT *book size* 24 x 30,4 cm

98

p.75 →

Mentalitäten
Niederlandisches Design
Prämierte Arbeiten des Designpreises Rotterdam 1993-1995
Securitas Galerie 7. November 1995 bis 4. Januar 1996

Colliers aus der Serie Passio von Ruudt Peters
Bei der Wiederentdeckung des narrativen Charakters von Schmuckstücken spielten die Ketten von Ruudt Peters eine wichtige Rolle. Amphoren und andere klassische Formen werden zu Bedeutungsträgern. Wie abstrakt diese Botschaft auch sein mag, so erhählt doch der Schmuck durch die Betonung des mystischen Inhalts deutlich eine persönliche Note. Das Interesse für diese Thematik teilt Peters mit Schmuckdesignern in verschiedenen westeuropäischen Ländern, die jedoch nur selten eine zusammenhängende Serie produzieren.

Pendants from the Passio series by Ruudt Peters
The pendants of Ruudt Peters played an important part in the rediscovery of jewellery's narrative potential. Amphoras and other classic shapes become the carriers of a message. Abstract though it may be: the jewellery acquires a clear personal meaning through this emphasis on the mystical content. Peters's interest in this area is something he shares with jewellery designers in various West European countries, who have however seldom produced such a coherent series as this.

Kabine für den DAF 75/85 von DAF Design Center
Das mobile Heim des Truckers verändert sich mindestens ebensosehr wie der Ort, an den er zwischen seinen Reisen nach Hause kommt. Die Kabine muss Platz für die verschiedenen funktionalen Elemente - von Cassetten bis hin zum Kühlschrank - bieten, die in das Interieur dieses DAF 75/85 einfach eingeklinkt werden können. Dieser Arbeitsplatz soll gleichzeitig ruhig und übersichtlich sein und dennoch eine charakteristischen Eigenart besitzen. Die grosse geneigte Frontscheibe sorgt für gute Sicht und Sichtbarkeit. Die schrägen seitlichen Fensterrahmen verweisen auf ältere Modelle dieser Fahrzeugmarke, die trotz grosser Probleme im Jahr 1994 inzwischen wieder voll produziert.

Cab of the DAF 75/85 by DAF Design Center
The trucker's mobile domicile is changing at least as much as the home he returns to between journeys. The cab must provide room for all kinds of functional modules, such as cassettes and a refrigerator, which in the interior of this DAF75/85 can simply be clicked together. At the same time, this place of work must be uncluttered and well organized yet still have a distinctive character. The large backward-sloping windscreen provides view and visibility. The sloping window uprights on the sides refer back to earlier models produced by this goods vehicle factory which, despite serious problems in 1994, is now in full production again.

Contents

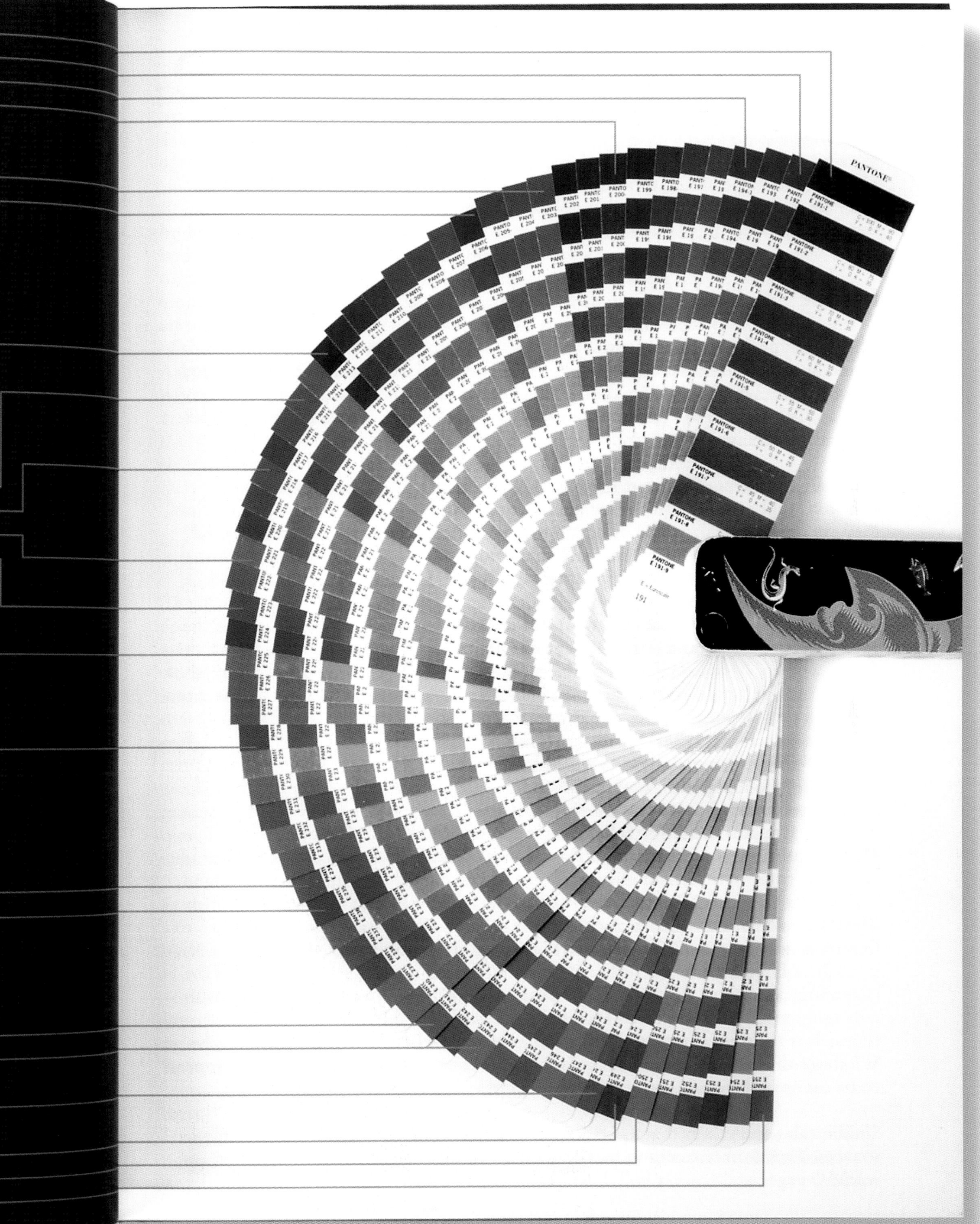

port betaald
port paye
Amsterdam
Pays Bas
proton
ICA
Amsterdam
Rozenstraat 8
1016 NX Amsterdam
The Netherlands
tel +31 (0)20 421 0769
fax +31 (0)20 623 2626
proton@xs4all.nl

Goodbye be Welcome
7 september – 19 oktober
Tiong Ang
Irina Balen
Dinie Besems
Clea Daiber
Ada Dispa
Hans van Koolwijk
Gosse van der Ley
Maurice van Tellingen
Luuk Wilmering
opening: zaterdag 7 september 13 – 17 uur
openingstijden: woensdag t/m zaterdag 13 – 17 uur
1e zondag van de maand 14 – 17 uur
Ada Dispa

APPLES &
best dutch graphic design
ORANGES
01

Amsterdam in colour

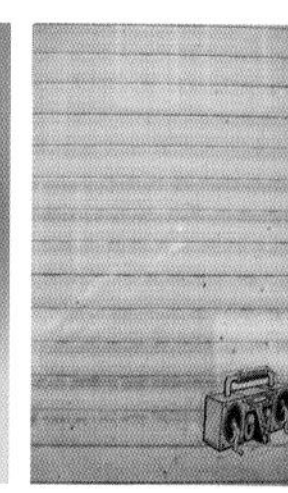

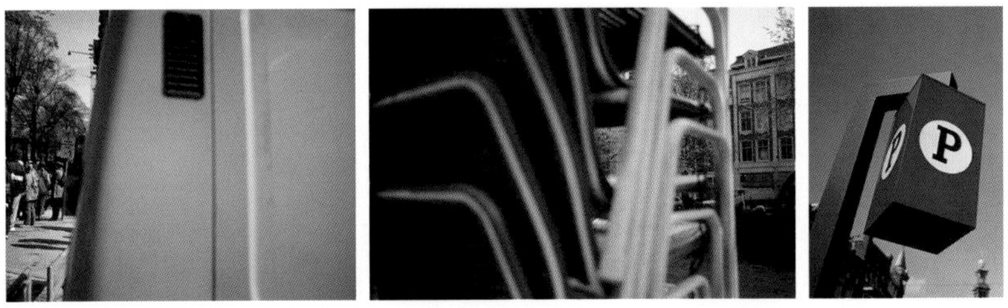

FOUR LETR WORD

SCAN
BAR-
CODE
HERE

FOUR

ETR WORD

HKIF ILLC GFAL BASE PGGA WAWE BOZO RXD★ MULE MK★E ★MHO LKQA GEFH R★OW XUHF AGEN MQSI YJYR HOME RUAN ARES XIBO NIDS UEGN TFHE JUDA MBGO FQIP LOID
CMO PHD★ REAL V★UH IZFC HAUW KNGE M★PJ GANT LGDU QIAT FOCI ★LQM ★USC JOKY CMIT EASE NUDE YONI DILL ★FKY MOPE CESS CXS★ UPXT MILO CHYH EMIR XAEW
SEME YREC RYAL SJUB IGUP PHON S★VV I★HD RADT VUST NAM★ XIII VQAG EMUS SORE BJED ★YRN ROTX FAWN KEN★ ★ZYL SREP NEX★ PUMR WEGR ANOJ USDI BYO★ DP★V
STYX DERR LUDS SLID DOEK TSIK SNUA QJFU OYGC ACVY PACA KLYL OAEV URGE QEUB SLEY QOPB BUOP SMEW PQYS EJWU VFMA ★YHR ERBN IVXD POLK ZIHM MORS ★KXL
HOER SAFE EMMA ACYL SRED ARYL JEKO AOCQ MUIR HARP HUIO ZBUS LOGP NOON FQH★ SEFK EWTA KIEX EQKC TAME V★PT WSVY RACK NYAS OALG YQKJ ZUFR UGYZ JAMB
ASHY SXIG JF★F ASAR MAGG MIME ULEX RGUG JINX AAWM RLWO WPK★ FEEL VHJU ADLF SMAF OPSO AOTM INLY D★KC YOOH YWNO RELY IJSE ALFS HGET BOLD VUFM WSEE
MH★X FUSE PCEP UQNQ STOP AWAY GPSA ★IYR P★VZ TOFF AGZO JHAX ★KCY YKBE ★SRL HINT BOMB HILA XFDU ZILT QOOQ CEUA ISMI BALA YYPJ XRUC K★OU ECLM MIXT
DGJA RINS FIQT ZLGI OFDH A★JS WAFF FYCW WAWS XBVA ★DAM YIMC MSTO GIVX RAWN MIST MBYN NKOY KOWS YUWN ★DWL RWB★ FIZZ OWQJ BALM KF★P REYF CLOD XSOF
NDMU WYTY LINN ARZG GPFU FEIK FIGS AFFY VIMS PCYP GFOR RNON KZYN BADS UMDL FOIN BEND MOES YPGT CHIV APJQ YWJH NQOG TOUN FATS NKIS JPEN FSDI KALE
JNZU OVCW ★HST ULNA GBAW XFE★ JGYX TRAY QWGO PTOL PELF EGGY OBVK SKID KEMP RUOU FORB QHEP ALAR AHCL ★BJ★ YFNO FIVA IMGN SQU★ MYGC YQXW FROM UYSK
CYNG BENS SHIR KOXC ARAS OQMC STYE YNEC YAWS BROO OULK JACK BGTI SNLY ★VJA TILL VDOA VCFU TZUB BUGS TYJJ PKGA ABET WSIK LOCK MLSU X★ZR EUIK UUWS
SUMO EOOM PELT LPOX EIMG PEON WARE EGAS TODY SXEC MH★★ VWDE MHUS ATLJ CREE ★NWN FEAG RIPU QAKP SELL VADE FUBS SKRY HGON JIZG COBS CLRE ★RZ★ DUAL
XCOA WYSO UOCP MIFR FLOG JOWZ GOLP SINH ASMM PILI HUTT OPNE HDUM ★KFP AUFW AHCU PRAD RIMA OOLG BRUH ANCE TNYQ XKN★ GIFQ M★XD ★LOH UCQI GIYS LMYH
BOSN ONNV AYUS SING SIDA RXAW HEPS THEM WEEM T★UZ CAMA IRES OONS GREZ TOLL CIOT FOBR ABEB OCWO I★ID PEBA MOBS EQBY ECHE BJOC RUGS IRID GOGO MOCB
YOHO GTNY JUMY RWUB BEDJ GEIW ONYX GITS ★MPO QM★J ASPS AGTC MEHG HDWI HATH DB★P WSYM GWYT XUUP UCJE OBFZ NACL EZCZ PYNS VELD PYES IGOB HEED ELQQ
DHEI PHDY SMEJ ON★F HYPE IOJH AMNX KIHO VEES LIME RY★W UZQS UPXQ GPOV ZERP KKME MNIM AINT CAHZ MOGS NOUP AIXX BPJI MIRK RLAB JWU★ BIXT DREW GUNZ
DODS SHOW MOED RAGS HOLT HUSS RAFT SEND VX★P PM★W WOPS BAAD IHKE CLAT KO★Z ZRRI SHOT VYLN WAKC Y★KB EUGE UFJM QIYV UNAG AEWV FYYO KCPU WIBP NOV★
BOOS U★DJ D★QP DHOB YXTO HOFS USBT K★BO BAWL TAWS TAPS DIED TARN C★YG JLR★ OCDL PEST CHYV BGYW OFFS JELL LOUT CATS FKIC SILT JGUC DXCI WAGS OYER
CXXE PYTK OJGA NOEK JOBE DIWA VKSU HKBY SMAK TAQ★ BIOG LGYN L★PS COPS UFBM LAHS NFTO RVUY ZEIU UWXY BE★B EWTS TATE IZST SASH MISS VVUE VDIA FENS
TYRO XQYJ SUCH SYAE CDNO ZYJU AMKS ★IEH OTIB NTAM KUKM JVOJ P★YS SAKY ZB★T YC★G TUSK WORM RCYJ JJAZ RT★H KEEM LSAJ BTQI MMOK HAAF UDTU EKWQ SB★P
LBDI BLUE VNIT VRNE KBJI UHBX ZIAZ ALIQ TANH UDHS EYGM PUGH TIME CHUD STIE GISM ITHN CORV OMRI FUCK OWYJ VETS UWJX OV★R ZYRJ ROGE IIVN TIGD EF★J
WAND CADI JDIU COLL SANG QUKN QZEB FFAO YMDH AJAR ALMT SG★★ BEEG DUSF ★DBR YELG Y★LF ★ZDU YMHY CNVU PXZA GJQU MEBB ITUC AFRU LUCE YTYD UTJ★ NUZH
DSAP PKOV ELS★ ★WYW SUNS ITGJ ZUSN FIPJ NITS CAPA LGXI IJL★ ENOW P★FF GOWL GWYY YHDD DAMP EMIV LV★O MYCA PICE EOXL UJZ★ QEBB WHAM HALF ZLUR PLED
SIKE VERS ROOS CUUY GCK★ FIAR FBWA AVBR R★YR YLTK ETPV MUSH MIGT UJWC EZLW IKSR DHOW RIZI CLEM DFAP DICT IUKT KOSW ERNI BDKE APOP LUAF MBAL Q★NQ
FBSA MEAD TJUF BOOB UBJE YOLD HULK LG★H OFJN POSF YHHG TAIX TUIS EFKQ PIMN MOW★ YZUW XS★J ZAUH MYOR POUR HYCD ZWOB AWXL MAWK EMM★ XWMY SQLE NAIK
OGE BERK TIDO KKMO AKES BAWN IMM★ KTOM ZROG PAXV SXET YXDK OHZC CACS SEMI YVCQ IIYC NANZ ETNG CT★F KLLE SY★O ZRUR OPTQ NIJE WDT★ RUTS BCXI SMEH
CILX GUWJ SUED KHOR OILY AXLE HNOX QYSH QROJ COCK NRYI HNZ★ L★VQ BAHS KOYH ROOF OQEV ZAQM AUUL GISQ BUUU VBOV UJHS BRIG VANS ★GUB UZAJ ★QRJ YNJS
VITA IJSY IWWK BOSH VMIU PQWU YAWN GIED NAOS HOAX QXIO X★XJ DGYX BYB★ APZJ DCMA LIGS JUDY DICH JOTZ FEGP EGQV ERRS EDXG KPEH CITE KXVO ZZ★L MH★J
MILT EYRX STEM GETA TEGG ZAMA FLAX TOLU BJYJ UDAL HZ★W HAJI SNIW GENU OJZU UPJA SOXX HZTI TAPE ZBAY ZKUS XLUK E★QK BLEB PECN RUNE VIDE QJFO GAUD
J★NO NCUM ROCS LAVE CIGT OABT JUWS BOGY QGH★ FUBO VCF★ FEES NAHS ENHP VOY★ YGJI GZ★Z USWM TINT GACA RO★A YVFV FYSK ZALF OBOL TEMS BAAS FZOA ★EVN
PALS NUKN HATS SLOB GAGS OCSL ★LIK UFGW ANON ALWO EJK★ UIMD ZONE NXOB YZYZ LOGS AIDA CQAG KAML XOFP ★IQP ★FDI STAG ★DKW FASH HM★D IOUK ASBY JUGS
UOLN SWLO ELX★ ZSAC KRIS OUPH SOMX ★JJL EITB LOWE RQVE KICK WAIF YJCT ZOWV BASK PERI LWOX ICEF GOGK DEKG VF★A RITS ★EGQ XBOL POWY PLIM TAEL EB★F
LVL★ B★RM ZEVP GJIL ESKY VIYO ERGA CQYA COAC BATE QIFT EJVW QSTE DJEV ★YGS FBUD OAFS SEVH TB★Q MATE TPBA BUYV SOIY WOPQ ★CML RETY YB★Z DGG★ ★REX
EUGJ COGZ PMUA ★SD★ BIAN ZXKI DIVI UPWB YZPZ T★ZL TFOK CWYE JGFU SPG★ KEBS JGIR ICWR SYLA ZZWU GHIO CUIJ XPUA SLUP E★LF GIRO IVJI ★★DL TUMP E★FQ
O★WX SWUM PAGE JFDA AJBE MALU TIRO ★HTR KITS IMBY HNYE AZOX APWZ VEFZ KOUP Q★KD PECH DULL RKUG YYQT AMBO VOCD DVIU KEYM ACPR HUTS MAAR ZIHW NHJO
MONG OAAT ZHOS DEED MWUU MCIM MRAM PYQE CPOP LEEK LYRE VEIN COAL DUNT TEEL VAGO CRAW WORN RONG QYUF JHTY GOAD ECR★ HARM AZIX YDFI W★XB GAIR POZK
YBCG ★EWF RIDE MONO MYPI YHEK WAWL LEKE NRVI YKKH G★EL QYUQ TKEQ COIR INIQ GANG IABF GLLA BGK★ HPYC AHDQ ETON ★BRO UVDU GOSS KPAA WEKE POQW NVIF
VATG FKHE ADDS FMWU MYNS ITES ORVV KEPS IWIS VLSI GING UWNU FNUK AOAC LIDO DAUD PLAR RIAS QPOF ECJK INXP OVPY MINA HEMP FEAR SOLS UCVP ★NXL KHYE
POZD UB★S TIES JBZU JCI★ TIFD ★FEL ZJYY N★KB TOWT WRCE MHKO JUTE HTVA OLIR PZUN ZINC CLIO GGSO SUNN KNIT VXWE LEVA VERB MEEH WERE CUNI XBMU PR★S
SEXY JBII UBDM HATE PTUQ O★GF ★FJY OJPG NPNU DAIL UYPV FLEE FYXC D★AF GJUS GBYN LADW CULM EDGY LKTY ORFJ AIJW TITS SDIC DOOK WTAY ADRY ACFU C★XG
EVDF KEWY KVCE MHJE TAMS ROOM GAMP DRAB BOSS DRAP CALX TOWY SPEC AMFU BHT★ ROTD DYWV UHWE AQVD NOIY EZJQ JMCO JXEZ OPUH EQCN AMXR UNHV EFBQ X★UV
JWNR YJOH LQEE FIRE NS★O LOOK RDCE OQLC MUSE DJVA NOES PEDS GBJ★ RAZM SELS DIEY INPH GNEK UNAU SXMO J★DO EPMX SLAV VUDT CYBN YHSJ FEER VIVA DTKE
LUAZ TIND SAND SPAA ZJXE KGFE UHZP F★OW FROG ★FJ★ DROP KX★B FORA ★HWS MLNA VUYC NONO FUND SIND AS★F KSAR XD★J VAKG UFWA VAXJ DUCK DNS★ YNFZ ADDI
FROW QJYN LAKH AUJR CARR LCBY DADO SCYE GKCE EAST NOCK DIXY FAZE BOEP KEOC PROD BDOL NKUP GNAI OCEW QCYM TOHO OAFZ OAKY OWKO DWIB LYMI OCAF TXZO
DREK XGHE GIBE LAIX KOAN URDY TRVU DOOS MRCO MONY TKKU HIEA ZJOW XACC SUJQ IMPS AXON UTOW BIDE NQRI GEOS BHUL MITE URIM FUSS KAID XF★J C★KB QITF
OICM LUTE GOOF YCXW GEAL WANY CIAZ LHYI AAVT C★AB NUTJ OJUZ JZ★D IMZW ★VJC ZMEU G★YX IFMZ OCJQ EWEJ FGNE KTUI XDGY YGVE CABS UVMB VARE FLEA GAYS
MKIH E★MX JIBS TOPI WOKE CHON AP★K PTU★ RUDE ECUN G★TT POV★ H★UZ WA★S T★RA FPUY SLED KQIS KZRU BODY CQJ★ PORK PROA KINO IRGX NKJA LIEN DULP VDVA
MXA★ KUIY MASS WILE DHLU QUYV POND AOBB TGOU DZHO RMOM OTTO K★PH CQKA VISA SAJP DALE RMYA JPVY FRET LOHQ YJCX PY★U ZMUU SOWP SPAY YIDS CXAA MOHS
JPEI VIVE XW★K FEEN MASH ★PBU DJUZ YBGC SAMH OPEL SADU QAMJ ZENS NMNA ZLZO OLEA LAME RUCK YR★G AEWN VL★I UWZO TACO VWRO OOZW KNAP PUEQ N★SP ★XMQ
XGJE UVAS GKLU SWHY CYHL BWR★ LIBR CAUF AGMS DEQY NGUY VFN★ BIGS HESP AMVD ELJU HQEZ MFAM HIRB BYJK ★J★W SILD SECH EWKS JXEX GCIW ABMR GOTO KAED
HWQ BEWV KEEN BOJI KERN QOFJ UWPW QUZH SURD TJAZ EPKL SUMP GUMS OPTS LEHS QKO★ GOES MUPT LAWO ZQAC XRUF KXUE COLE BAWJ PIES DII★ HYIW JNIL BFTY
KRSO VABO SOLO AGYR TANA YZFQ OXKY PEES OZPB TDLE URCC WI★Y WXER J★KI MMAC WARM ★WVB ENEW YUCA URUS JQ★I YTQB UWXT ARTS FWTU FLAM YTJR YYJL RJIH
HF★G SAID UXLF DOWD TGOP ORWV NGBO ANTI FINI ERS★ WGYN EYID XMUV AUDM ASMU EEID UZVY MOVF RWZO SOFT HEAP COME SIDE GEYU FJ★B XMY★ ★ROB ETCH SOYR
ZEYO VAIR PURI YINS Z★CP SOPS VYSD SGAX KEFS CXYU YSCR LX★★ OQDJ SUQS UVAN OPXQ I★YM SBK★ FIMN CLUR VKRA HIZZ BLOT SCUR BAZW EDEN ODYL D★OX MFEC
KUGX SBB★ CANN HURM JOTA PHBY CYNW HEAT BZEH OAIM VHSU UYYB ILYS PUNA M★ZW KEDS AWVU UPDW NOUT RILL XOWR LAPS ★ANN JUDP UMXK QUHK LAWK UFIV IDZM
YAUW STOW IIIX LIRA QTWE CLEG PIBK SIYM DVIJ ANDT ZYTU YHUC TOPS NUBS FWUN YWP★ HYYE YTFI ★DWC HMAH FHQE ★LRL BLAB LOKI WS★U MELT ★MMJ ABZB B★LW
PIHC UT★W CEV★ GALS JOMO ZZYA ★NBU MIOT XELL CUFI IYLX BORE SPUR PLHU PIPY IXHB FFII OWMY HARE B★IC PQAS DYDY YTAL AENR HEBE DUEL WTIN ODOX NIZX
DAUB HAPS CLOW ★IDN GLEI ZEHC VKIJ IFOS EPSN FYZK YIWB SETT MAUL WPKY ABSB PARM DEEV TQZE ZYBX ALAS CIZE ZUMX AEIR GEEK ★XAX WZES VV★X ★BKB MUON
VCHA AASD RUSA ESJL U★KB ONLY YELT RRPU QFKI GAYH TDIP B★UZ ★LRB JETS FBOB NOMI TICH HOVA OL★M MOOP JESU CVAZ MLLO IRHW EJGW IMHE RANI PUBB TATH
KDYA YPUD KSAY RISP SAWS BADE EPGK FIND JEWS BET★ XOIH HLXO WBPO RDIF PDFO SXOJ SICK XGAT PARR PBMO UBHE WURM SXAN SALP FOXY SPIV EUWJ QDOS QWIL
EXPO YILL BIOS GCES BINS OFLQ OPPO ETUI ADDC NDEL AOLZ AXLG SAB★ BAFT UCEG PIER DYED HQNE ★WTB CC★T KEWK HERD WART FJIU EFTS BENT FIDO VUYX NAPE
NHN LEAQ DORF ROTS SDHI GFUA ★HHW ANAN JOCO HOPE AHNL ZZUZ FAZG GRIG ROCK XFIZ HPDE OIRG UEWC JUYJ EJUF WAIN ZZOV HWRA KILD JUDS NYDL ★KX★ LABS
YCSF CRAP RUBE IAJG YHZP ★RGG ZDXE TYU★ EYED UEHZ QWGI ECSW SYND FALX FHTO GEOX YUKY EFXC SOGU POUF UHEZ GG★S RGL★ BOHB AUZJ ★QQR ZM★P FELL KDYJ
OATH AVER ★HNW C★UZ CRIK HHQA NABS GVYC GUTS YIFK SMOG HEUA LINS HZUH UVTH EHFU CAAZ OONC LIED DANK SBGU TYJC JANE MAID XKIM MYFQ L★TN ★HR★ ★DQT
NCRY FUOI DUKE NIKP CITS KNAG SOVY OWNS XSUD IPP★ KHYZ SO★N R★SV CUSK TBKY C★ZF ★★HF BLYE BQDE QAEE KEGS QIOE AMCY IVVR PFHI DFOY COHO SROQ NEMF
HECK GAFF YYCJ PAEF SUKS ELLS RATE DIME CHAS QUAL BYSV NIDE KC★P WU★Q WDEA VNLO SAGA HOUR ★UBQ DUCH GLN★ WHLA RXAP TALK PPXY VEES DOTH FOID VIDW
GRDO OUYL YCYH HWNO KMOA EAUS PMOC LKEU PEIB XTAL OYSN WYPB IMTO KECU BIBS INZQ WREC ★NMG KQEI BSYS IXCY MMIX JSMI OQCU FDTA GLOP TFSI Z★HE KHBO
CAVY MYNA VKZE SGAK XJOH YMTR NUPG D★OT MICA PROM V★ZR AQUS VESC BTDU FUST YKOH BENE DIKA TAVR SLOG CURN DZOU UPAS RJDO YPF★ YEND ZONA GIRR CAOA
ISMY AAWR YPIL OH★T RRYW QXOF GIEN WXB★ MNHO ★GON ADME ZEBQ RAMY BRIE GTJ★ SUET IXNH DD★O INCA QEUG JILT ACDM GNV★ HOLI ★ITK JERK DENE AREW ALMA
PV★Z ALHB VURV QQAI DOGS ZX★U BLAE HOPQ ACZB UQQW QFEX JMOU ODFI ★QPB CTYE JEFF XOYH MODE TRIP GZOI BLGU DOCK EXRT BOOT UD★R XJUM VIVW REHS DRMI
IPFQ SEEL BXJ★ GYVR ABLY AIBX PEYO UCNJ DB★H XU★M TINY AMPS AFYH VNUA OZGI PBAY JE★D OWCV LVIH AUHG YYMS FYKE Y★OX ★MJU Y★AF JELU ZSAZ QEJH OTMU
FWSE NOPI IPCO GWYW HASH YNBU WLOH CRUX FLAT LXLE DF★H GOOR TODO LEXW BUBN VUUA EFIM IPHT TGYZ UPEW AVMG NPDU CISB NFAE ANIL FRAU SPAR HGAB LUWY
YTIV HAIR HQAI OWES JADZ KEPT IRJE ★EUC USMM BAIL ZVHA AVLX AKYD SHED IDEA UERJ ITVB LOSH POZZ TWAE RANK ZMP★ WURZ QIFR TARO VNAY YOUX HERM JGAI
TD★S TRAP ELTS LEZZ ★YLV EWAQ NYSY BITO OVUG SHAY E★CB HEND RYVE WIMP DURA TVM★ ★BVQ UHDL MYJN JROI EUOI XMIX HLES RBWI IDVL GZKA JNGA ASEV GINN
TOBE BHOI ACRE YUPS MIRV PLEN FAIX WGYE YQNF WOVE OYKG WGVO XBHO RGHA OWPA BIGG UCCU YHED YFLL VQDI AZDJ EVRD ORFE WESU RENS RKEV KCAG TJEG TRJE
GBOI XYGY CZIF HQQE SILK JUYK SORA MYVF KGNE REDE YPOS YLMK OSOR ZXKY DEMY FWUK PISE AMYL FOPS ★GUQ YESK TOLD IPCU JUVU EALE U★VM YSXS OWCO EZGM
BVYY QUAZ T★AM YP★W EARD FOZY AJQY RNAV ★VMB PENE HKKA XLDU JOUR QQ★A OFVF YHTE YOSK DOYA BACH LAND INFO OZMS UKTO HEYS RAAY KEYZ FBRU UJOW AZKC
JX★P PSDE CYUU SNUB AGEE RBAI FCEF J★TU ★RP★ EYAS KXBU QT★D ELLS MILU FIQC BISH COAX DISH ZTHO EVER RR★T MDJU BASD YJUR DELI RAID YZZO WTUC WOJT
PUCG ★CGO PEIN OGRY F★★O FLH★ HXEX C★OZ UCUS MKBE UNMU DAOS FUNS UUOF SOON CC★K GNJ★ BIOY PISH PHYD BEBF DOOL FHB★ ABBE AUTO RAZS MPHA YIRD AEJT
CEEK UNKZ JOGS UTVV MZI★ GEFY MING ZJIS BAFB SYZF NEFI MLI★ FURY OXXE NTAC AG★S PE★U RQTY GRVY AUEW TODH VELA YKBQ OIZZ KIHK DL★N QAYD WDOW CTAG
EG★Z TALE BYJN GUTD ACHY ALUM WW★M JEMT WW★O MQRI M★OB GHRO YHFD XP★E WAKE INKS NRVO VUOW XWAY FVDA BERI QKOM RAWS QHNU EKPQ MIEN HUGY AWBR ALKY
XOD MIYL CQAZ GRP★ GARS FOAP PAXY IOFX WQYP ISRE BCAH JFUQ AQDF HURT UNCI ★ZG★ WTEW VYUO BYKE ELSE J★CP QMIB UGYM BURN FLEY ★PCX RMLI ANAL QMJ★
RINK ★OSG GGOX YU★K OZSE KFHE MWUZ SILO MUYP ORZM ★LGD POOL FVAM IUHG JLYC FDDE XOIJ R★MA PYOT QMVY BRYD IQTP MH★C ATAP YBG★ WQO★ DARG AQQN BARB
L★AL KZQI GINS AWNS MZOS HOJG ★VGL GA★C LRR★ FNS★ KUKU ASQT L★S★ TOUT DOIY QKAM CLEF KNUR KAIF HI★K COWL ARHW XHCI EGJL NIDI CAKE LBAD YXHS XXHA
JOQT BALI QYLV DUYB PACE DOQN LQKY CLUB ★OJW UTIS HVKE SVUG K★RX ALOE DOOM ILIR QRAX COOM U★RK CSQE DEYC K★VO UQZK UBRC ODDS RIMS HULE SPYE DALI
EMPT IFCZ EMUM MXBI SJGO ARBA Z★WQ VLIJ KX★K REAK CL★Q NZD★ AOES TOUK OUWP XAPH WKUY G★OB DOWP ACME CVEK XTUP QODS VEGA CFQO TAP★ RPY★ HYI★ EMJG
GOLE UBYZ ★RIG HAET GOFF QYIE JASN GICV ASBV FLOP RQKO QUWI ALAY UT★X GKHU FURL JOMI VARA OXFN PAND LOBE OQWF LD★N IXQT DCEI THIB KURN YJPQ MOTC
MATH TRUH JURN VMDY SM★U TIPO HOLM RSCE BO★O RYQB ★URS ZMPA UBAC REND RKYQ KAME PYW★ DEFY GYEQ ★★OK OFPJ FARO SJBI GEFG MIT★ MARS AZYM NAUV B★YK
RVDI COTS JYSR QAYE FEDS SOZL NAYO ORDT LAIC NWQ★ EOAD YNWM RJSO R★OI JSJ★ PLEJ LUGS TOJW ODES LJRI NSVI SEAN AUNT LOUL VEKQ BKAI RCVE BAKB FOOD

FOUR LETR WORD
FIND F★CK FACE

010

logo for - uitgeverij 010 publishers - in helvetica

010

logo for - uitgeverij 010 publishers - in serifa

010

logo for - uitgeverij 010 publishers - in cooper black italic

010

logo for - uitgeverij 010 publishers - in textile

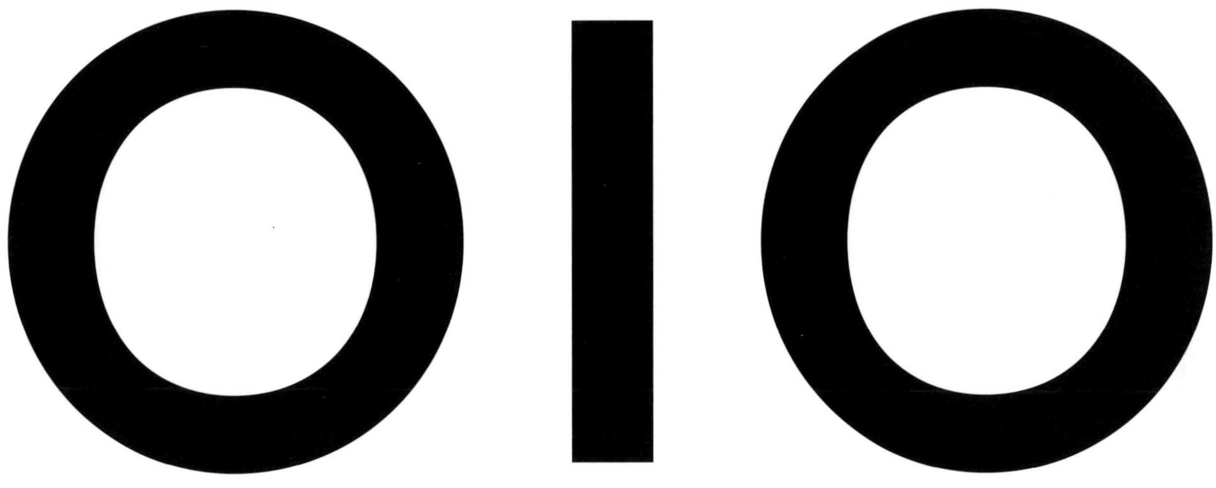

logo for uitgeverij 010 publishers in avenir

the logo for 010 publishers (zero ten) is a simple formula that can be applied to any typeface: type oio and erase the dot on the i.

richard hutten

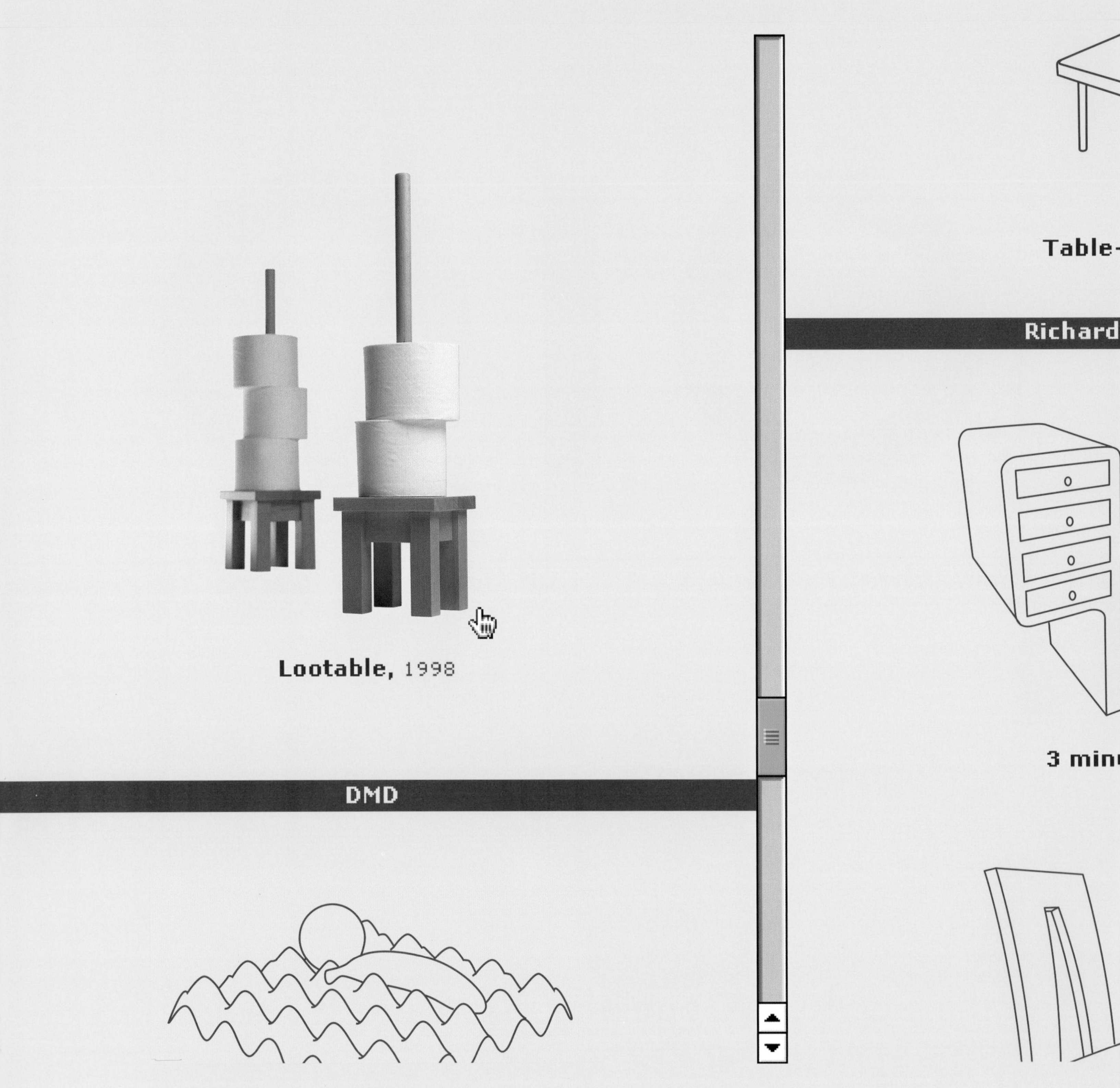

1999

n Studio

spaces

Richard Hutten Studio
Centraal Museum Bookshop
Centraal Museum 'De Refter'
Thonik Studio

Richard Hutten Studio

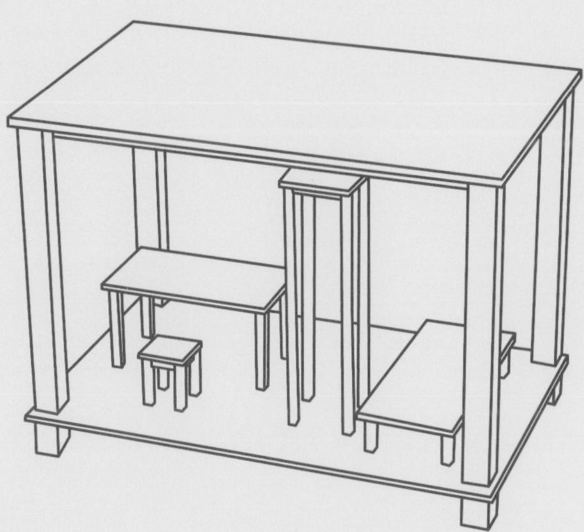

Table concept, 1990

contact information

SCHORER STICHTING

SCHORER POLI

SCHORER BUDDYPROJECTEN

SCHORER PUBLICATIES

SCHORER HELPDESK

SCHORER INTERNATIONAAL

SCHORER OR

SCHORER VRIEND(INN)EN

SCHORER BOEKEN

SCHORER CONSULTANCY

SCHORER WEBSITE

SCHORER HIV-PREVENTIE

CMYK	PMS	ZWART/WIT
100 M 100Y	PMS RED 032 U	80% ZWART
50 M 100Y	PMS ORANGE 021 U	50% ZWART
100Y10 M	PMS 108	0% ZWART
50C 100Y	PMS 375 U	40% ZWART
80C 15M	PMS PROCESS BLUE U	70% ZWART
70C 70M	PMS VIOLET U	100% ZWART
30C 90M	PMS PURPLE U	50% ZWART

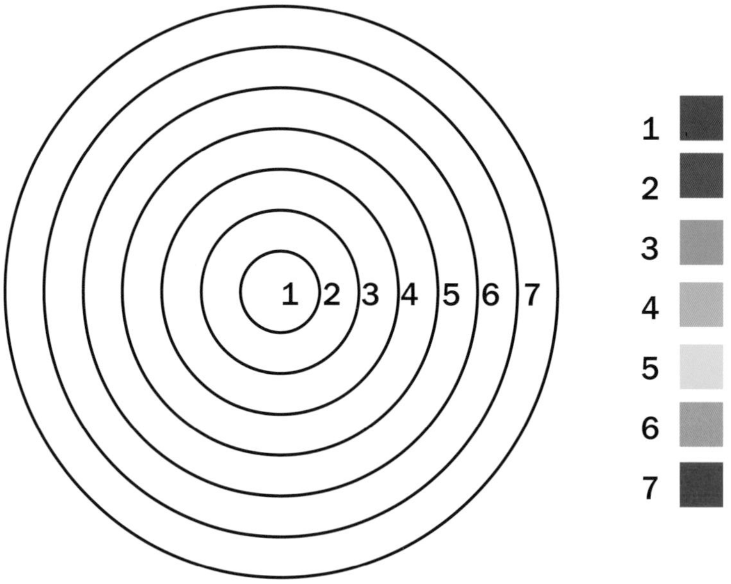

1 2 3 4 5 6 7

1

2

3

4

5

6

7

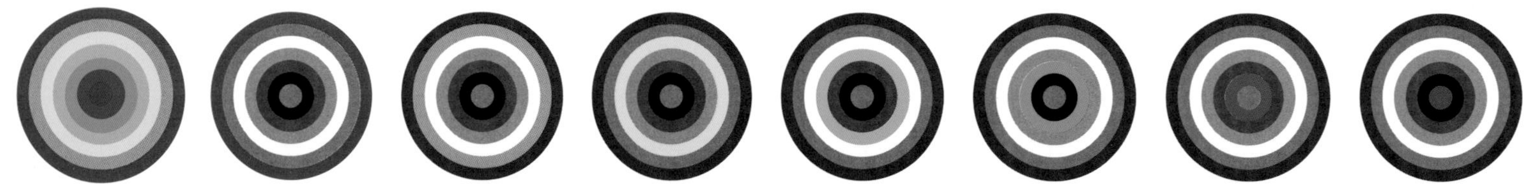

De bende van Leopold 

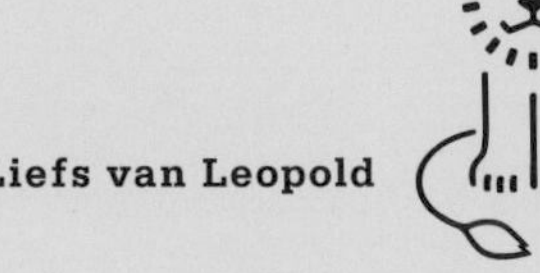
Liefs van Leopold

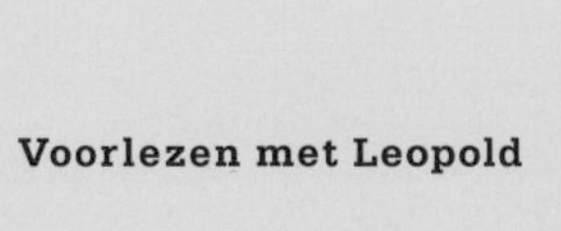
Voorlezen met Leopold

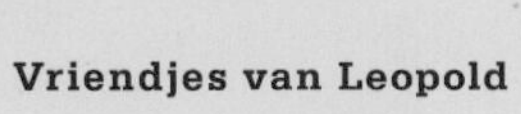
Vriendjes van Leopold

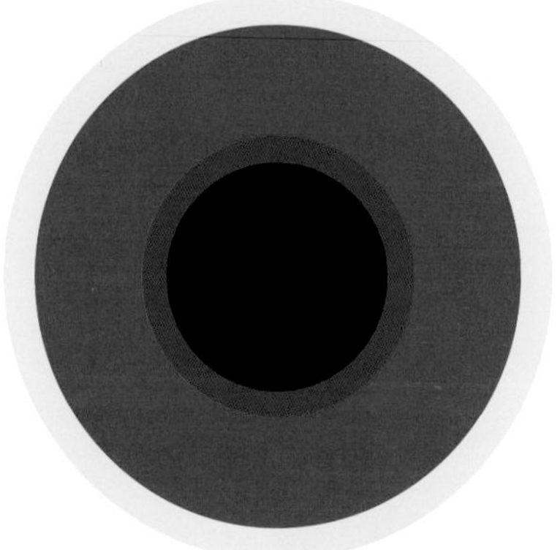

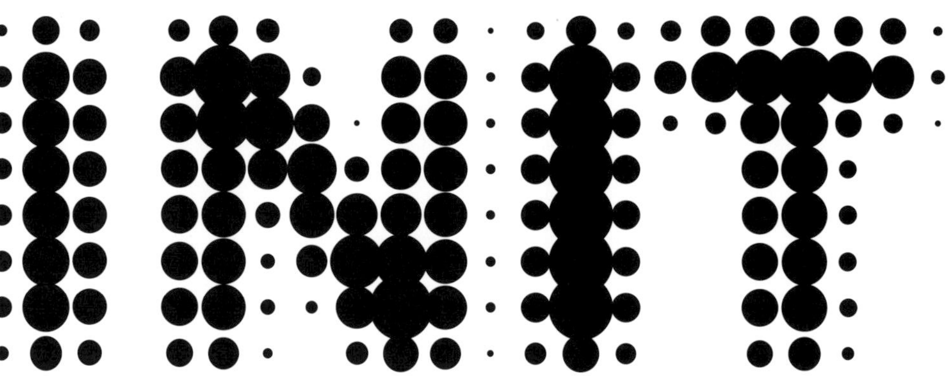
INIT

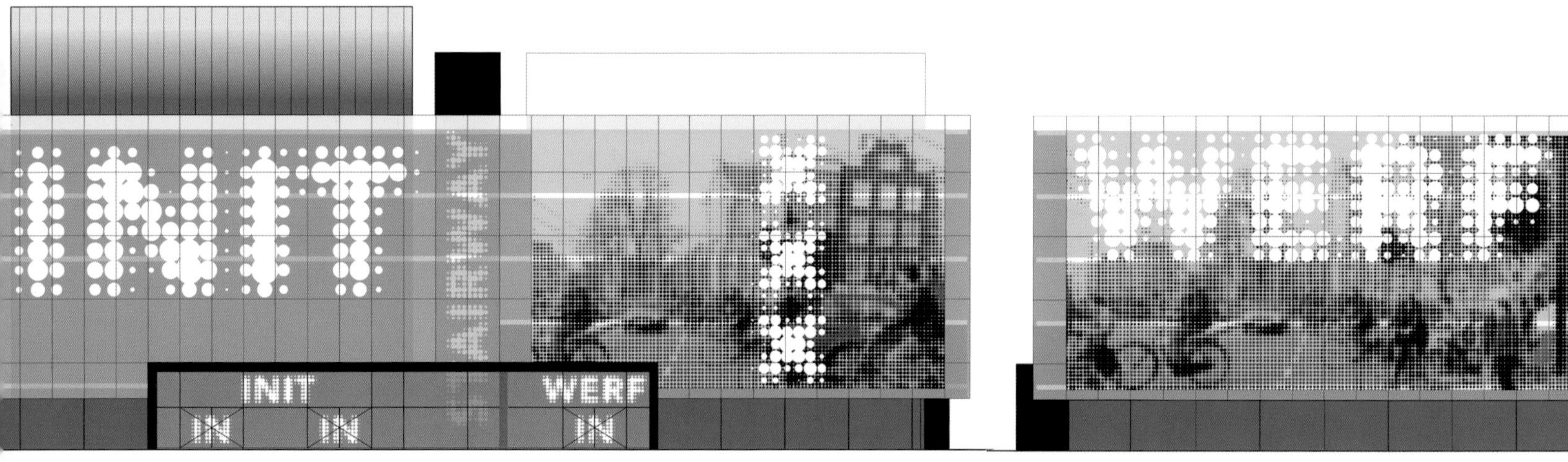
INIT
STAIRWAY
INIT
WERF
IN
IN
IN

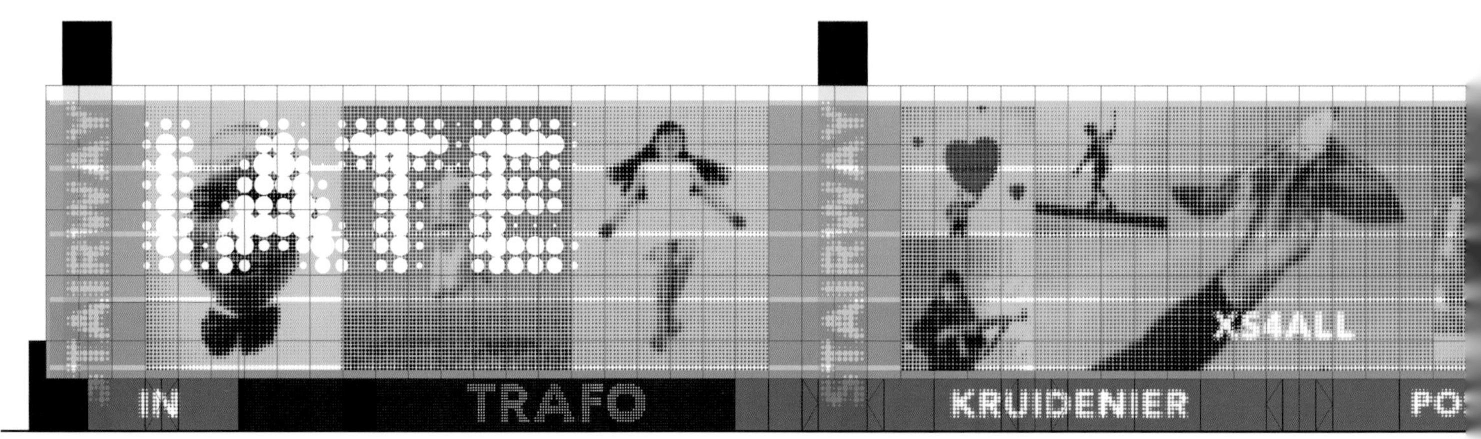
STAIRWAY
STAIRWAY
XS4ALL
IN
TRAFO
KRUIDENIER

1996
dit
jaar
zochten we
Raad
bij een
Cultuur
hier is een
verslag

(10) 'Dera dema meperewerаaaaa,' imis ajirin. (11) Po jamer jamer jamer. (12) Somor tokoro ajiturumer, ajemesira isimeren. (13) A jiram isi, ajemesira isimer ero, a tam ero, andiseren.
(14) Aondijur ero, a tam ero, arakam aondajumesen. (15) 'Ah, tia, aikon, biria, jakane pokomer. Boondi. (16) Jusiwir ovogaisen. (17) Jakar jak ajowa tok aoweren.' (18) 'Der dema
meperewera,' imis ajirin. (19) Tam andipeseren. (20) Po jamer jamer jamer.
10) 'I want to see for myself.' that's just what he said. (11) He paddled and paddled. (12) He arrived at a village, and spent the night with them. (13) That night he slept, and after spending the night, that morning then he departed. (14) Going to the river that morning they spoke to him.
(15) 'Ah, son, brother, don't go. Come on back. (16) The man with fire isn't there. (17) That man, stays at a river.' (18) 'I'm going to see for myself,' said he. (19) That morning he departed. (20) He paddled and paddled.

I - B DECISION

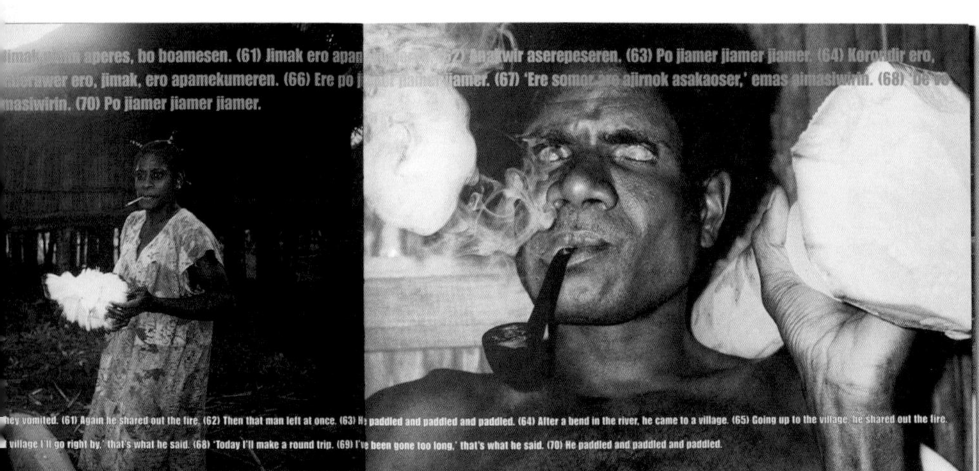
aperes, bo boamesen. (61) Jimak ero apan
Anakwir aserepeseren. (63) Po jiamer jiamer jiamer. (64) Korondir ero,
ero, jimak, ero apamekumeren. (66) Ere po
jiamer. (67) 'Ere somor ero ajirnok asakaoser,' emas aimasiwirin. (68)
masiwirin. (70) Po jiamer jiamer jiamer.
hey vomited. (61) Again he shared out the fire. (62) Then that man left at once. (63) He paddled and paddled and paddled. (64) After a bend in the river, he came to a village. (65) Going up to the village, he shared out the fire.
village I'll go right by,' that's what he said. (68) 'Today I'll make a round trip. (69) I've been gone too long,' that's what he said. (70) He paddled and paddled and paddled.

IV - C BACK HOME - ROASTED FOOD
(1) 'Der simir!', Pinim emas feak mewerer, arer simir bo bo
aweserem piamim,' imis ajirin. Bo avur bo amer ero, a somor jis akujermeririn.
(1) 'My dear old man!' As soon as he got the smell, his old man vomited. (2) He went up to the village. (3) 'What's the matter with me
(6) After people vomited all over, he put fire in the village. (7) After setting out the fire, I always ate things raw.

'emas ajirin. (3) 'Da pok dir andeamem. (4) Der a jimak aram
Kokowar, der mejerewer, 'emas
A somorjin meter aimeweremes ovogaisen. (9) 'Ya, de
meperewer,
in. (10) A vuris jurorem
kuhmantukmer ero, birmoro ajekamter ero, ti an
My dear old man' said he (3) 'We always eat things raw. (4) I'm going up river and look
Kokowar, is
that's what he said. (6) His son was a real brave. (7) If he's going way up river, that takes
couldn't beat him. (9) 'Yes, I'm going to try it,' that's what he said. (10) A stick of 'vuris'
In a small
(12) After putting it in the small mat, and after tying it up, he put it in the dugout.

I I I GETTING THE FIRE
(1) Serependirimer. (2) Ambisen ten diramer, diramer diramer. (3) Ambup
Anakw
tairimer. (6) Teme
Jimak si si
si, tejemsejirimen. (8) Jemsejirim ero, avuruserem ajemerteren
ero, kokejomseren
ja tairimer, tairimer tairimer.
(1) That morning he departed. (2) He went down to a sand bar, he went down down down. (3) In midstream he follow the current. (4) That man
straight to the house. (5) That morning he ran, he ran and ran. (6) He entered the house. (7) The fire was burning burning, burning
continuously. (8) While it was burning, he took the vuris wood. (9) As soon as he got it, he quickly ran back. (10) Careful that the fire didn't go
he ran fast that morning, he ran and ran. (11) Careful that the fire didn't go out, he looked back. (12) Careful that the fire didn't go out,

(3)
er a awerserem? (4) Jisaima jepnak pokorem. (5) Dijuamima
(8) 'Der pokdir dawaimis
(5) It has been a long journey,' he said.

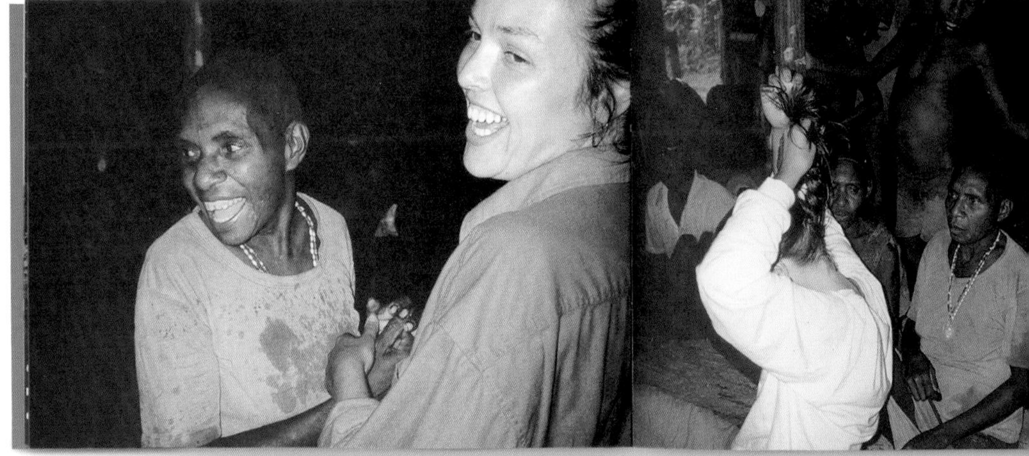

18 12 '93

watch, which I had hidden away in the inmost pocket that I had, and had forgotten when they began their search.
They seemed concerned and uneasy as soon as they got hold of it. They than made me open it and show the works; and when I had done so they gave signs of very grave displeasure, which disturbed me all the more because I could not conceive wherein it could have offended them.'
These observations stem from 'Erewhon', the topsy-turvey utopia of Samuel Butler, published in 1872.
The narrator of the story crosses a pass in a snowy mountain-range, and arrives in the unknown country of Erewhon. At first the inhabitants behave friendly and hospitable. Things change after the discovery of his watch. The chief magistrate who is in charge of the investigation of the visitor, suddenly shows signs of horror and dismay. Initially the narrator surmises the usual reaction of savages who have no experience of European civilization. But soon he discovers that he has misinterpreted the expression on the magistrate's face. It shows more hatred than fear. When a short and stern harangue is of no use since the visitor doesn't understand the language of the country, the magistrate conducts him to a large room, that turns out to be some kind of museum.
'It was filled with cases containing all manner of curiosities - such as skeletons, stuffed birds and animals, carvings in stone (whereof I saw several that were like those on the saddle, only smaller), but the greater part of the room was occupied by broken machinery of all descriptions. The larger specimens had a case to

80

themselves, and tickets with writing on them in a character which I could not understand.
There were fragments of steam engines, all broken and rusted; among them I saw a cylinder and piston, a broken fly-wheel, and part of a crank, which was laid on the ground by their side. Again, there was a very old carriage whose wheels, in spite of rust and decay, I could see, had been designed originally for iron rails. Indeed, there were fragments of a great many of our own most advanced inventions; but they seemed all to be several hundred years old, and to be placed where they were, not for instruction, but curiosity. As I said before, all were marred and broken.'
At last they come to a case containing several clocks and two or three old watches. These are compared with the watch of the narrator. Again an indignant speech is delivered but, due to the lack of mutual understanding, it has no effect. Only when the narrator puts his watch in the case with the others, the magistrate calms down a little. He seems to understand that the narrator must have taken his watch with him without any intention of violating the laws of Erewhon. Anyway he does not get condemned but is treated generously by the inhabitants.
What kind of law has been violated by the narrator?
At first he thinks he is suspected of contrabanding: maybe he has accidentally evaded the usual tolls of the country. It is only after a long time, after having learnt the language and after getting used to manners and customs, that he discovers the real reasons of the magistrate's anger. Some five hundred years before his arrival the Erewhonians decided to destroy all

81

eternally yours
visions on product endurance
010 publishers
eternally yours

de Volkskrant
OP
MAAT
m.c.
ESCHER
culturele
weekagenda
donderdag
10 september
1998

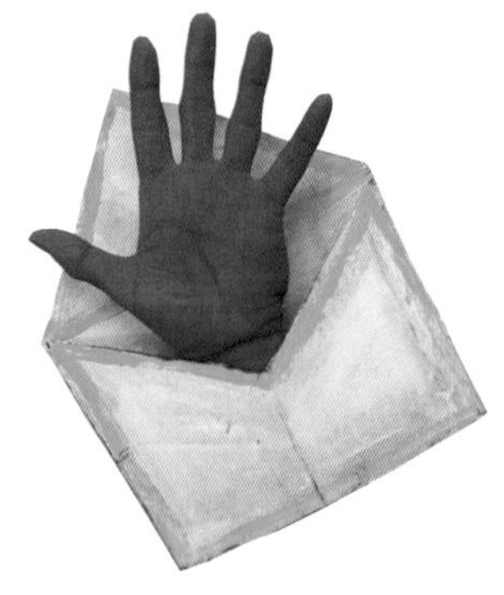

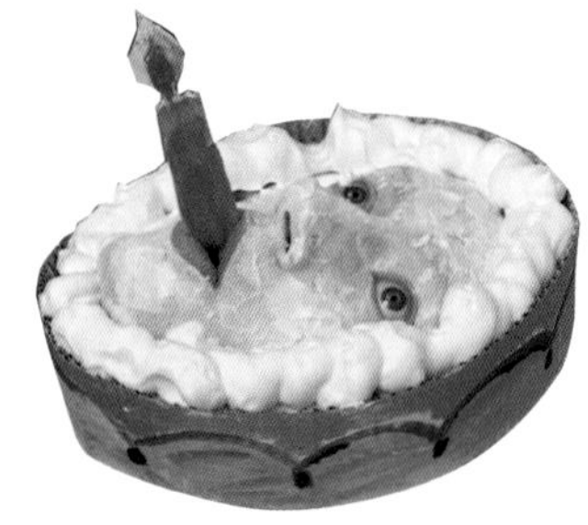

plak een sticker van je keuze in het rode lijstje op de postzegel

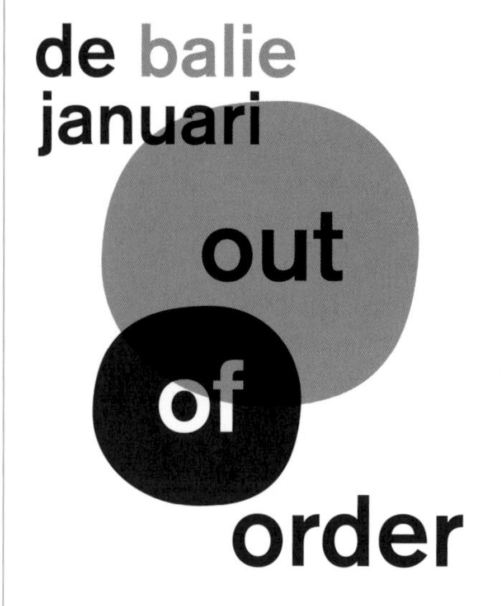
de balie
januari
out
of
order

de balie
februari
lef
leefbaar

de balie
maart
quick
&
dirty

debalie

debaliedebat

debaliecinema

debalieuitgeverij

debalietheater

debaliecafé

Gemeentelijke Dienst Afvalverwerking
Jaarverslag en Arbo- en Milieujaarverslag 1998

Afval is het begin

Wat overbodig is of kapot, wordt weggegooid en krijgt daarmee een nieuwe naam. Dan is het plots afval. De oude functie of waarde is verloren en daarmee begint een nieuw leven. Want wij gaan aan de slag met alles wat niemand meer wil hebben. Daarvan houden we zo weinig mogelijk over en we halen er zoveel mogelijk uit. Zodat het weer een nieuwe functie kan krijgen. Met afval begint een proces.

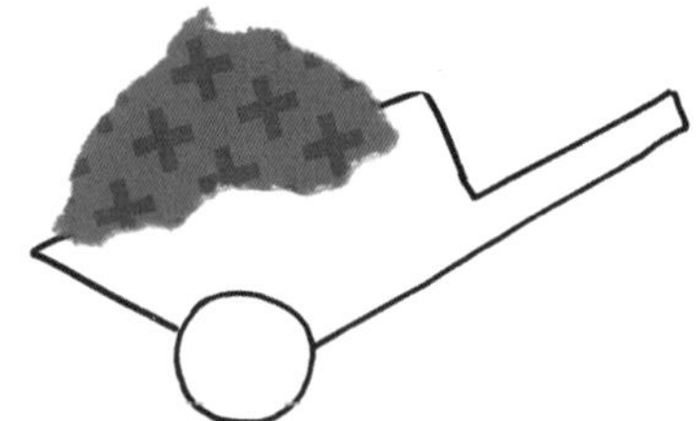

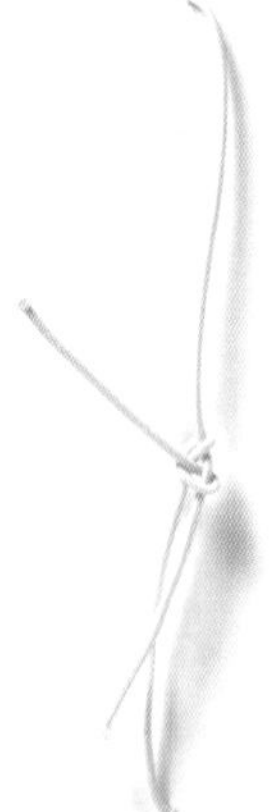

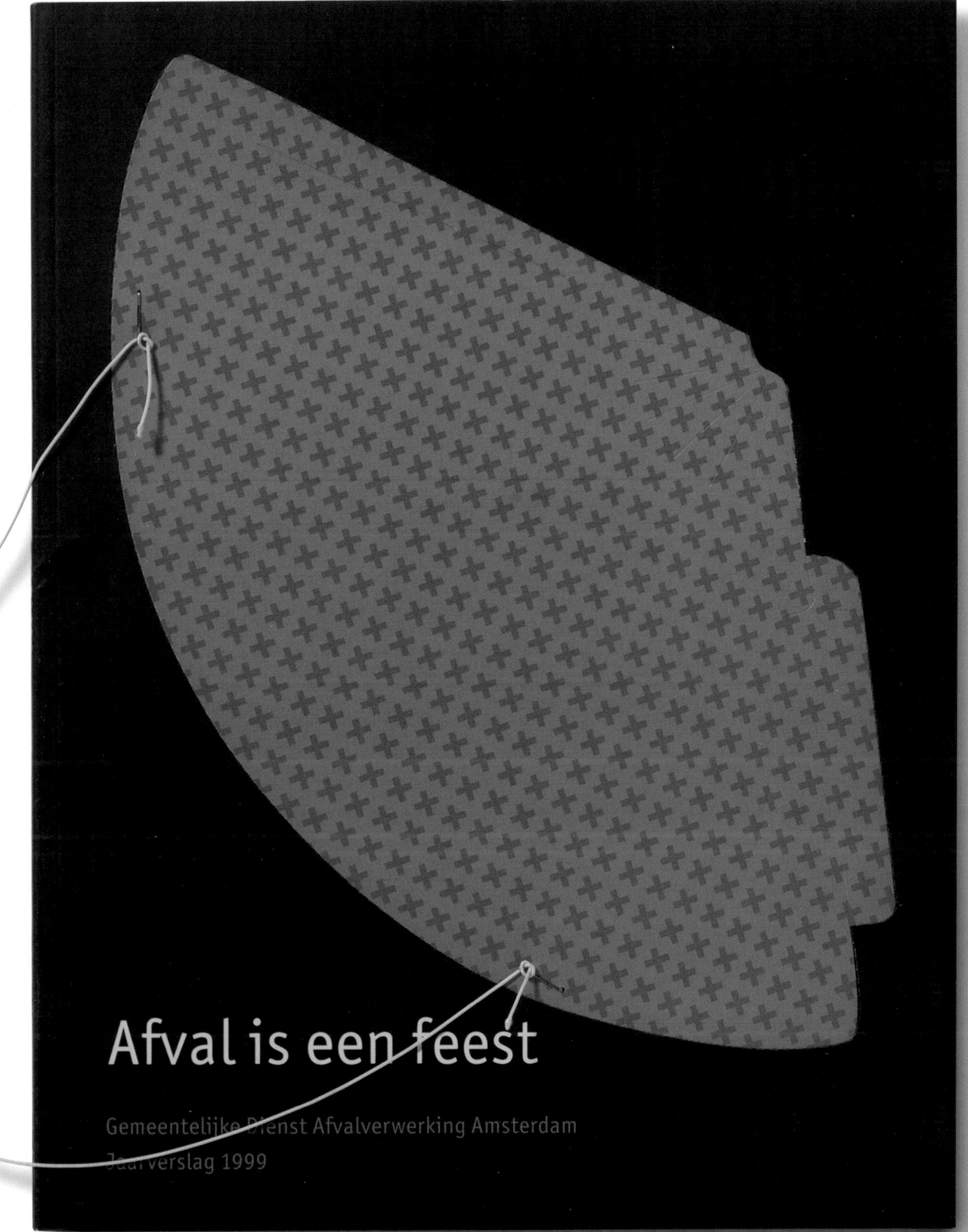
Afval is een feest
Gemeentelijke Dienst Afvalverwerking Amsterdam
Jaarverslag 1999

Locusfocus

987654321

Sonsbeek9

123456789

Locusfocus

987654321

Sonsbeek9

123456789

Locusfocus
987654321

Sonsbeek9

123456789

B5OKKS
THE CATALOGUE, 50 BOOKS, KESSELSKRAMER 1996-2001
*They say that a week is a long time in politics.
And in athletics, a tenth of a second can feel like a lifetime.
But in the arena of advertising, 5 years is the blink of an eye.
*This catalogue contains 50 books in one large volume and tells
the complete story of KesselsKramer, from 1996-2001.
*Read the whole series to find out everything you ever wanted
to know, and some things you possibly didn't, about the
creative communication agency based in Amsterdam.
*Guaranteed to include examples of almost all of KesselsKramer's
work along with in-depth reviews, comments, stories and
interviews with some of the best minds working in advertising,
design, architecture and communications from around the world.
*Take a detailed look at notorious campaigns like ONVZ,
the infamous Hans Brinker Budget Hotel and less well-known
work including Boylan's, Bol.com and Oor. You can also follow,
step-by-step, the birth of new brands like the Dutch mobile
network Ben and KesselsKramer's own brand 'do'.
*Now you can make your own informed judgement about the
agency that has been described both as "15 years ahead of
everyone else" and "a one day rumour".
*With a total of 50 books in one chunky set, there's something
for everyone!
concept and design: thonik*, Amsterdam
(formerly studio Gonnissen en Widdershoven)
B5OKKS
5OKKS
The complete collection of 50 KesselsKramer books and more!

B5OKKS
KESSELSKRAMER 96-01
KK SAYS (HELLO)

KK SAYS (HELLO)

PART 02
THE STORY OF KESSELSKRAMER
A'DAM
Europa Regina
Advertising in a Multicultural Society
Change the script
Brinker Experiences
The future of television
NOW A BED IN EVERY ROOM
ON AIR
Make friends with brands.
Instant access to today's alternative brand creation
Edited by H. Remark & J. Koa
do FUTURE
Contemporary History of Het Parool
The sudden recovery of a Dutch national newspaper.
PERSONAL ADS.
PART 01
THE STORY OF KESSELSKRAMER
LONDON
FREE cab
kkloves grass
Brand Reincarnation
MINDSM
the world. KesselsKramer meets
Shaping
How to launch a new TV channel.
COMMUNICATING THE 5 SENSES
CREATE YOUR OWN MEDIA
NOT POSSIBLE!
TIME FOR A COFFEE KLATSCH
The story of one company and its favourite beverage
Usage of animals in advertising

KK THE HUMAN Story
Product Design in Communication #1
Product Design in Communication #2
FanMail
INVASION OF THE PUNKS
The United Nations of Advertising
PART 03 THE STORY OF KESSELSKRAMER A'DAM
Eye
THE MYTH OF YOUTH
KK SAYS HELLO
ideas
The Jukebox of Ben
50KK
IDEAGLUE
Kill the deadline the new face of a newspaper
A MIRACLE IN WARSAW
The Changing Workplace in Europe
14
365daysofe-mail @kesselskramer.nl
REALHEROES

enfestiv
grachte
enfestiv
stival gr
festival
festival
15-19|8|2001
grachte
Gemeente Amsterdam
ING

grachte
prinsen
arcadi volodos, piano
engrach
tconcer
20e editie
rt prins
18 8 2001
nsengra
prinsengrachtconcert 20.00 uur
kinderprinsengrachtconcert 17.00 uur
Avro
HOTEL PULITZER
Amsterdam
SHERATON
ING

N.T.
NARCISSE TORDOIR
Z.T.
NARCISSE TORDOIR

Overzichtsfoto Installation view
Tentoonstelling PSK
Brussel, 1987

ennucommedesgarçonsennuann demeulemeesterennucarpediem ennuikennujijennudenieuwecollec tieennuuitverkoopennuetmainten antandnowundjetzt....

DOG TROEP

n8

1ab

rotterdam

1ab

rotterdam

2e
n8

2e
n8

Kosuke Tsumura

made in japan

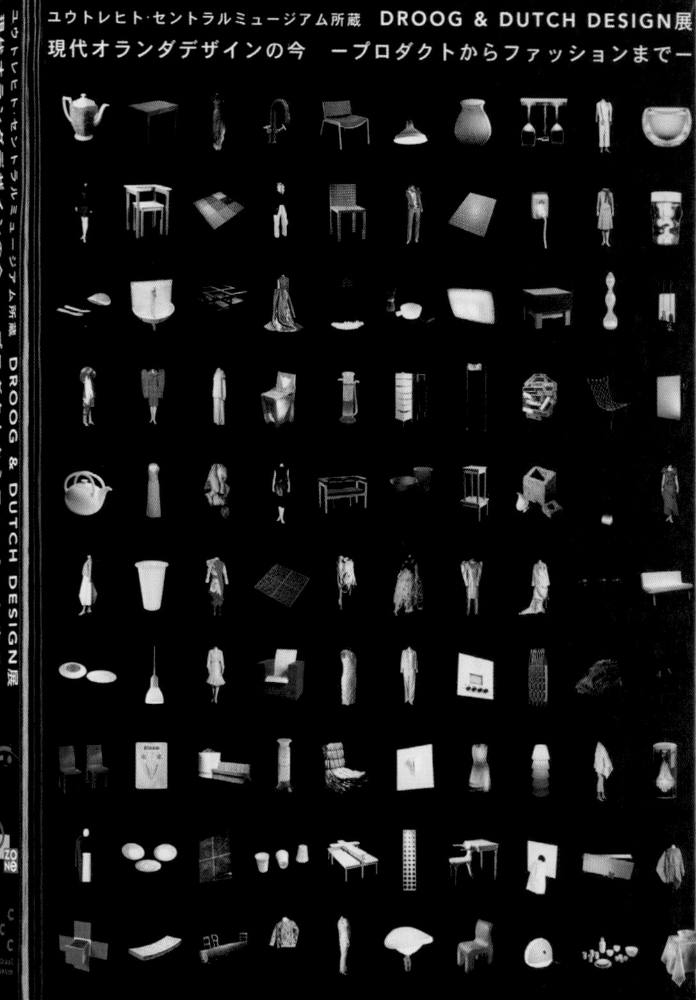

う。卒業して間もなくの１９９５年、イエール婦人物コレクションでグランプリを獲得しました。たまたま婦人物のデザイナーのパコ・ラバンヌがその記事を「リベラシオン」誌で読み、アジスにパリで行われる婦人物のショーの前座を飾る機会を与えたのでした。以来、講評や新作紹介の依頼が波のように押し寄せましたが、冷静に、量産可能な実用的紳士婦人物コレクションの開発に努めました。「もちろん、まだ何年でも屋根裏部屋でショーのためのコレクションをデザインし続けることもできますが、実際に着ることのできる服をデザインし、売ることができるようになった時初めて、ファッション・デザイナーとして存在することになると思います」と彼は語っています。

１年経つか経たないかのうちに、アジスのブランドはマーケットに登場し、東京、パリ、ニューヨークで販売されるようになりました。ショーは、アムステルダム、ウィーンで開かれ、１９９９年7月からはパリの紳士物モード・ウィークにも出品されるようになりました。

programme of his couture show in Paris. A wave of publicity and offers for new presentations followed, but Bekkaoui kept his head and retired to develop a portable men's and women's collection that was ready for industrial production. Bekkaoui: "I could of course continue in my attic for years designing collections for shows. But to prove your reputation as a fashion designer you need a portable collection, that you can produce and sell in series".

Within a year the AZIZ label was introduced to the market and it was sold at once in Tokyo, Paris, New York and Japan. At first Bekkaoui presented shows in Amsterdam and Vienna, but from July 1999 he also showed in Paris during the men's fashion week. (JT)

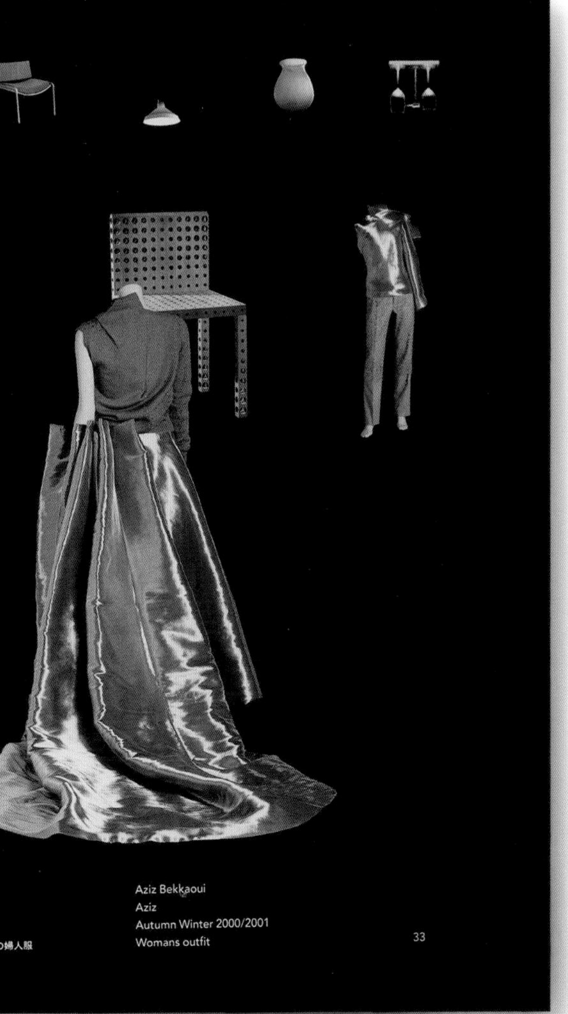

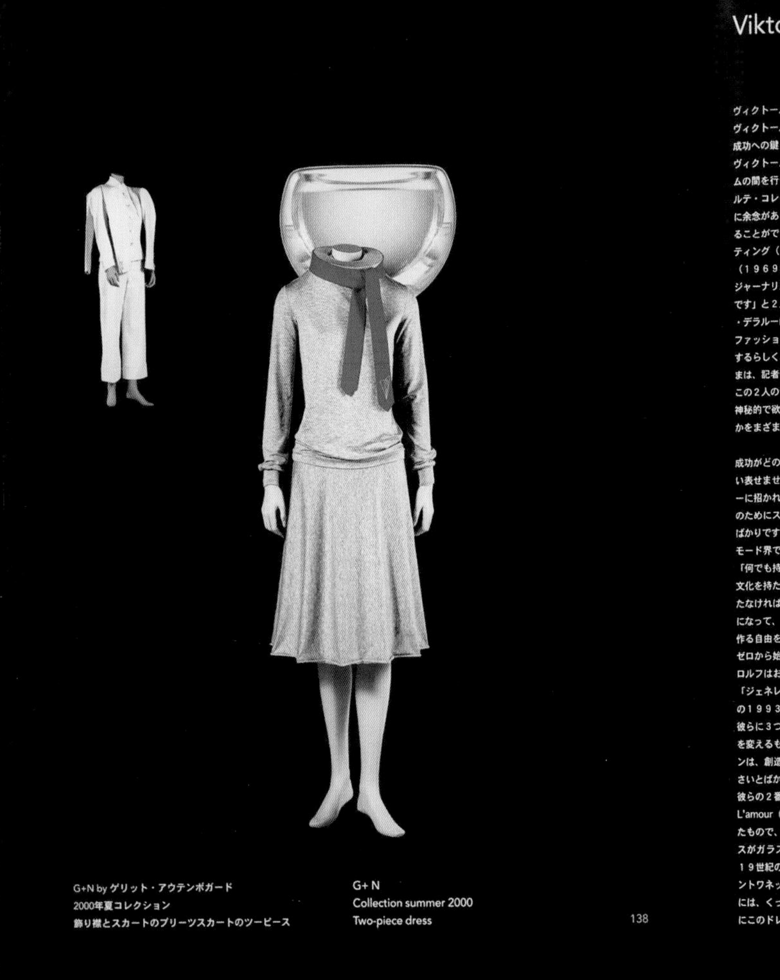

Viktor & Rolf

ヴィクトール&ロルフ
ヴィクトール・ホルスティングとロルフ・スヌーレン
成功への鍵
ヴィクトール&ロルフは、フィレンツェとアムステル
ムの間を行き来しています。彼らは、2回目のプレタ
ルテ・コレクションと5回目のクチュールショーの準
に余念がありません。選び抜かれた最高の招待客を迎
ることができ、わずか1日の間にヴィクトール・ホル
ティング（1969年生まれ）とロルフ・スヌーレン
（1969年生まれ）は、200名ものファッション
ジャーナリストを迎えました。「こんな経験は、初めて
です」と2人を古くから知るジャーナリストのニコラ
・デラルーは言います。「ヴィクトール&ロルフの服は
ファッションエディターにとって魔法のようにアピー
するらしく、先を争って服を試着し注文しているありさ
まは、記者会見というよりショップに近い状態でした。
この2人のデザイナーたちがどんなにすばらしい方法で
神秘的で欲望をかき立てるような宇宙を築き上げてい
かをまざまざと見せつけられました」。

成功がどのように2人に変化を及ぼしたかを一口には
い表せません。最近では、編集長アンナ・ウィントゥ
ーに招かれて、アメリカ版ヴォーグの2000年6月
のためにスティーブン・マイセルによる撮影を済ませ
ばかりです。1993年から始まった2人の協力体制に
モード界での大きな成功へとつながっていきました。
「何でも持っている人は別として、例えばファッショ
文化を持たない国からやって来て模範とか手本とかを
たなければ自分で作り出すしかないでしょう。彼らは
になって、その経験がまったくのゼロから自分の歴史
作る自由を与えてくれたと言うでしょう。“まったく
ゼロから始めることは本当に素晴らしいことです”」
ロルフはお気に入りの作家ダグラス・コプランドの小
「ジェネレーションX」から引用しました。イエール
の1993年のフェスティバルのためのコレクション
彼らに3つの賞を与えましたが、そのことが彼らの方
を変えるものを持っていたかもしれません。コレクシ
ンは、創造の自由のための叫びであり、どうぞご覧く
さいとばかりの規格破りのとても隠喩に富むものでした
彼らの2番目のコレクションは、題して「L'hiver de
L'amour（愛の冬）」。パリの近代美術館でも展示さ
たもので、舞台には白いゆったりとした舞踏会用のド
スがガラスに押しつけられています。半分に切られ
19世紀のシルエットは、まるで断頭されたマリー・
ントワネットのようでした。「芸術とファッションの
には、くっきりとした境界線などありませんが、モデ
にこのドレスを着てもらった時、そのドレスが舞台上

Samen op vakantie v.l.n.r. Hans Hagen, Madeleine, Kees Preuyt (1932)
Hans en Kees (1932)

èsGs

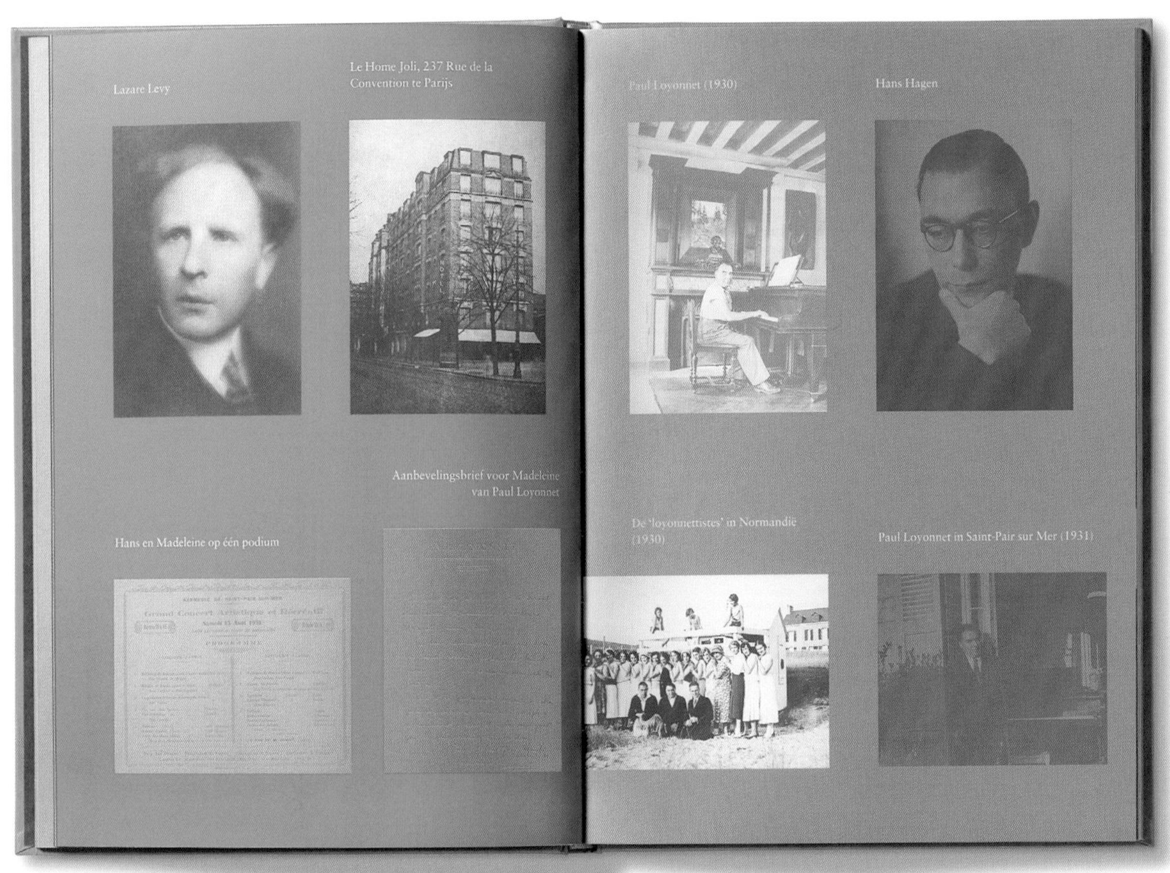

-ciété Gavigniès

De stervende is in zijn
ruimste vorm een vogel die
in versproken adem vliegt

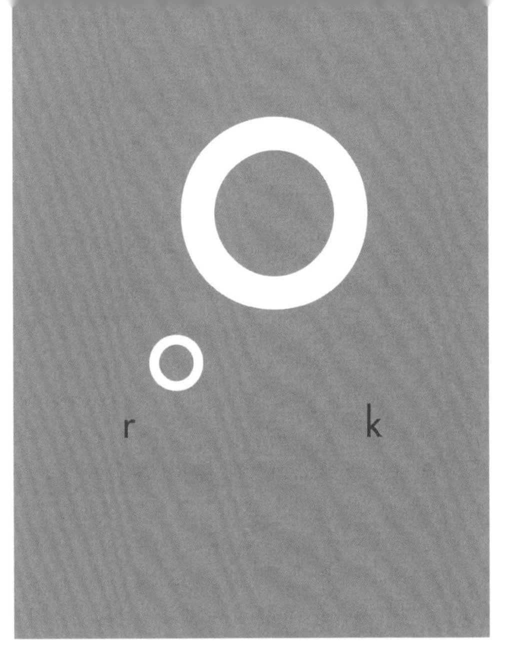

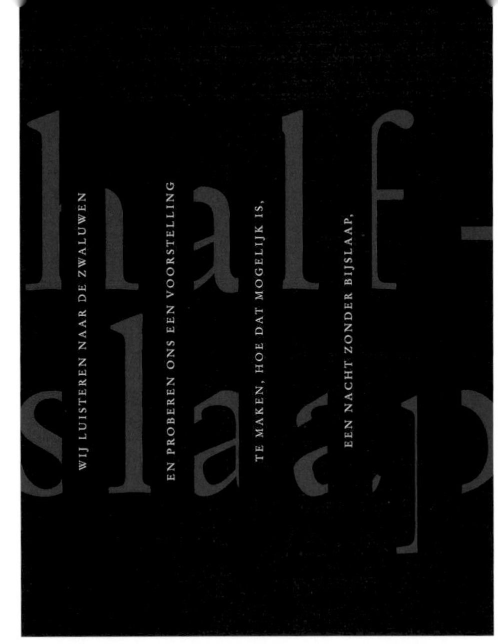

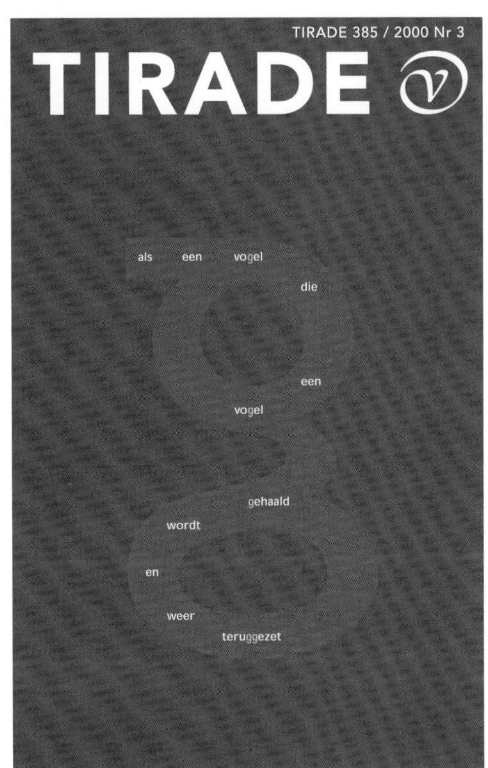

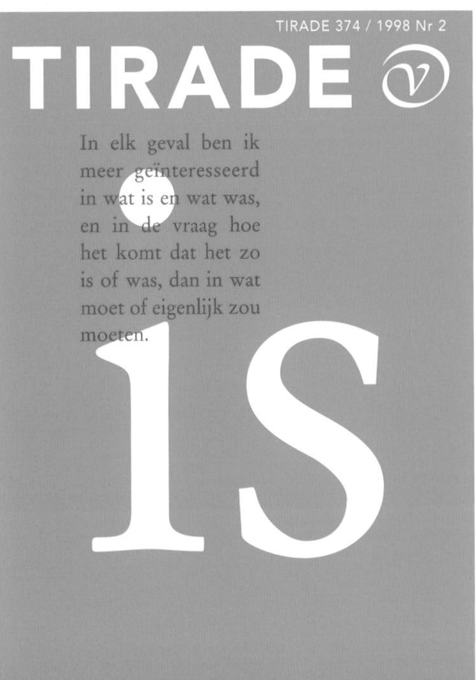

BASTA 1997
BA
ST
1998
a yearbook of
contemporary art
in the Netherlands
jaarboek van de
hedendaagse kunst
in Nederland
TA
20
00
jaarboek van
de hedendaagse
kunst in Neder-
land
TA

uitgangspunten voor het cultuurbeleid 2001-2004
CULTUUR
ALS CONFRONTATIE
OCenW
Ministerie van Onderwijs
Cultuur en Wetenschappen

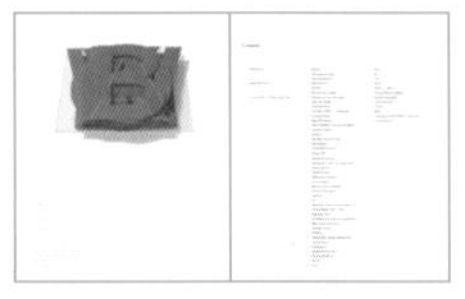

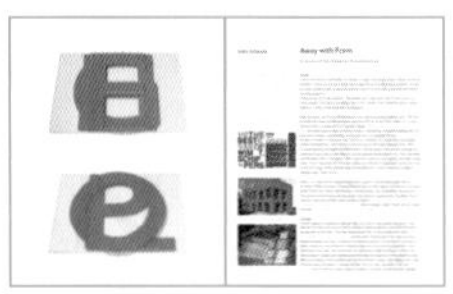
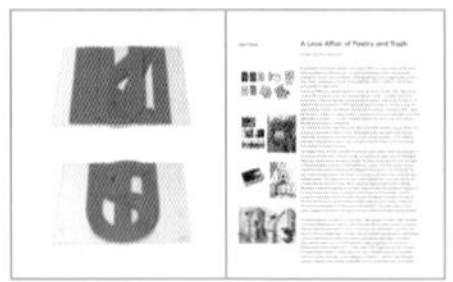

Vedute 2001, pp. 2, 4, 8, 14
Vedute is a project in which artists, designers and architects are invited to express their own views about space in a '3-d manuscript': a three-dimensional work to fit into a space measuring 44 x 32 x 7 centimetres. Our entry employs the 26 characters of the alphabet. The alphabet represents space because of it's endless possibilities to create meaning. We selected precisely the right format capitals in our favourite Avenir type. To create the three-dimensional effect we chose two- and three-millimetre thick perspex. Twenty letters three millimetres thick and six of two millimetres would fit precisely. But which to chose as the thin letters? When we considered the six letters of the name Avenir we discovered that they are extremely evenly spaced in the alphabet. We made these transparent, the others orange. They are stacked following the sequence of the name Avenir: ABCDVWXYZEFGHNOPQIJKLMRSTU. Our alphabet fits precisely in the required size.
client: Vedute, Gitta Luiten, Suzanne Styhler
project: 3-d manuscript
photo pp. 2, 4, 8, 14: Wim Beishuizen

Peter Kok holding De Zingende Zaag no 20, that had just come from the printer, while Ruud Douma, Thomas Widdershoven and Coen Mulder try out the game that became no 21.

De Zingende Zaag 1992-1999, pp. 20-21
Poetry periodical the Zingende Zaag is made by poet and artist George Moormann. For a period Thomas Widdershoven worked intensively with him on the production of some twelve issues. Each issue had a separate theme that dictated both content and form.
De Zingende Zaag nos. 16 and 17 (bottom right)
Title: de parabel van de kringloop ('the parable of recycling') . Theme: Ecology. An issue in a cigar box, a box for storing anything and everything. This tranquil volume was immersed in a vibrant collection of recycled cigar print-work with which fellow artists responded to the poetry.
De Zingende Zaag no. 18
Title: trek ('appetite'). Theme: Appetite, travel and desire. The life of the common eel was the leitmotif. In addition to poems, this issue contained a picture section cut across to allow a combination of stylised drawings. The drawings were of eel-like body parts – brains, intestine, fingers, penis and related abstractions.
De Zingende Zaag no. 20 (bottom left)
Title: op de rug van de hemel ('on the back of the sky'). Theme: Inspiration (or the Flight of Plato's Soul). The cover showed an absolute cliché: a poetry album picture of a butterfly. One side of the pages was not cut open. Spines in the inside pages were the result. Once cut, the pages showed Coen Mulder's images of weightless symmetrical spaces.

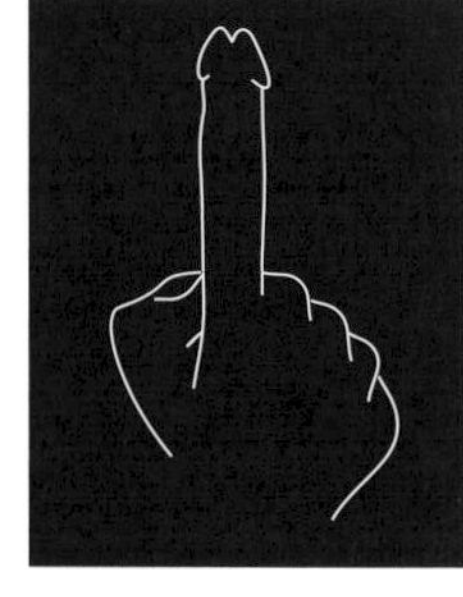
De Zingende Zaag no. 18

De Zingende Zaag nos. 21 and 22 (bottom row, 3rd from left)
Title: zigzag. Theme: Poetry as child's play. The magazine was disguised as a game which, in addition to presenting the usual poetry, also presented a playful way of writing real new poetry.
De Zingende Zaag no. 23 (top right)
Title: de gelukkige schrijn (the happy shrine'). Theme: Relics. The original copy was presented as a sacred object. A carefully designed reliquery was made to hold these sacred pieces of poetry. The magazine was a fascimile edition of the box and its contents.

A wooden shrine was made – and carefully lettered by George Moormann – to hold the original copy of the poetry for De Zingende Zaag no. 23

De Zingende Zaag, all inside pages of issue nos. 24 and 25 on the studio wall

De Zingende Zaag nos. 24 and 25 (bottom row, 2nd from left)
Title: het koekoeksnest ('the cuckoo's nest'). Theme: Manifestos. De Zingende Zaag, normally devoted to poetry, opened its pages to a clutch of cuckoo's eggs: the violent prose of the manifesto. But this was a far from quiet nest – giant letters proclaimed: DE ZINGENDE ZAAG. Folded in book form this produced pages of black bars with prose weaving like a mountain goat over, under and in between. The entire inside appeared in miniature on the cover (legible with a magnifying glass).
client: De Zingende Zaag, George Moormann
project: poetry magazine
publisher: De Zingende Zaag
printer: Spinhex and others
special thanks to: Peter Kok, Ruud Douma, the poets, artists and designers who contributed and of course the printer and all the friends who helped binding, folding, sticking etc.

Centraal Museum 1996 on, pp. 22-37
Utrecht's Centraal Museum is a highly decentralised museum. The five collections – old masters, modern art, local city history, costume and design – each have their own atmosphere and are managed relatively autonomously by their curators. One of the tasks of the new

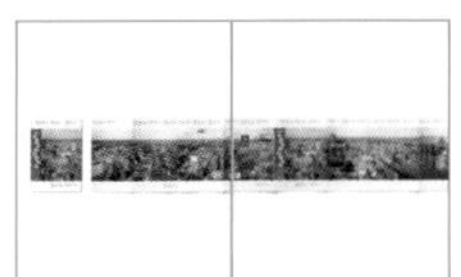

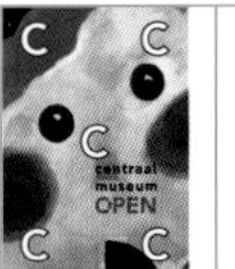

Head of Presentation, Ranti Tjan, was to increase the overall recognisability.
We suggested developing a new logo. This would form the key to the museum's diversity. A key that would be expressed in the slogan: 'five collections, one museum'. The logo comprises five c's one of which is in the middle – central. It is immediately recognisable, while at the same time it involves a minimum of design, making it easy to adapt to the museum's wide range of activities. In some house-style items the logo is open rather than compact, the c's being in the corners and the middle. The identity programme accommodates smaller identity programmes that play with the c's. Sometimes they link up with the text, as in the with compliments slip. For the CM Club, the b was made with an l and a mirrored c. For the Kids Museum a new typeface was invented, the c-style, using c's for all the curves.
For the re-opening of the museum in 1999, following a major rebuilding project, a c was transformed into an o, for open. Printing this on the existing stationary and envelopes created specific items for that occasion. Repeating this several times resulted in a loud headline effect. And enlarging it in combination with colour produced a poster.
For another poster that was part of the opening campaign we wanted an image of a face with the letters OPEN in eyes and mouth. It looked like an Anthon Beeke type of image so we asked him to make the photo. He gladly agreed. We were even more pleased when he proposed his daughter Borinka as a model. His family has modeled in his work as we have in ours.
client: Centraal Museum, Ranti Tjan, Milou Halbesma, Sjarel Ex
project: identity programme, opening campaign
printer: Spinhex
photography: Anthon Beeke
special thanks to: Borinka Beeke

Comic strip for Centraal Museum Newspaper

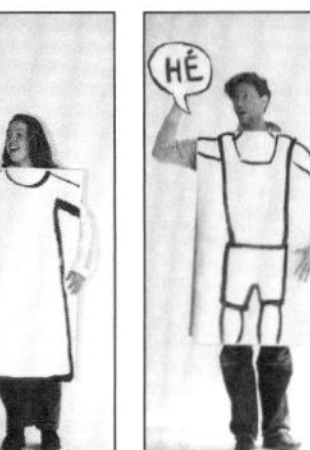

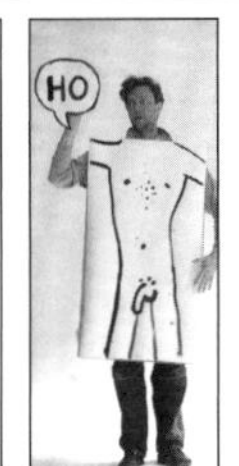

Panorama 2000
Panorama 2000 was an exhibition designed to be viewed from the highest church tower in the Netherlands – Utrecht's Domtoren. The objects were arranged in the streets and squares, on façades and roofs in the inner city. A central aspect of the communications programme we developed was the typographic image of the exhibition title. The letters and numerals of Panorama 2000, placed at different heights, form an undulating pattern. Some are upside down. Vertically, the image resembles a spiral staircase – displayed in banners hung around the tower.
A prominent feature of the Panorama 2000 identity is the colour magenta. This was the first time we actually dared identify a show with one bright colour. Later, we gave two other outdoor shows colours: Over the Edges

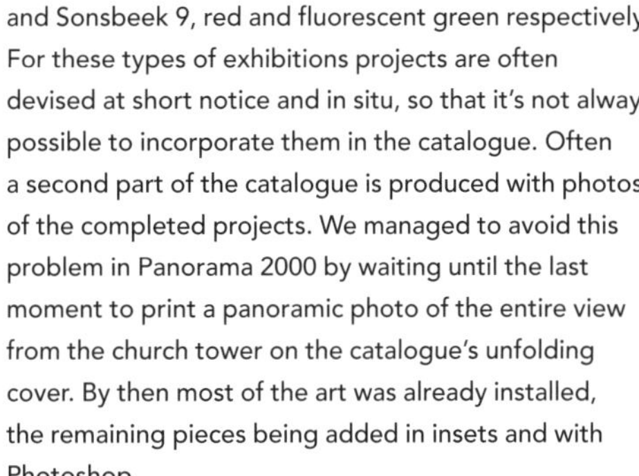

and Sonsbeek 9, red and fluorescent green respectively. For these types of exhibitions projects are often devised at short notice and in situ, so that it's not always possible to incorporate them in the catalogue. Often a second part of the catalogue is produced with photos of the completed projects. We managed to avoid this problem in Panorama 2000 by waiting until the last moment to print a panoramic photo of the entire view from the church tower on the catalogue's unfolding cover. By then most of the art was already installed, the remaining pieces being added in insets and with Photoshop.
client: Centraal Museum, Sjarel Ex, Ranti Tjan, Milou Halbesma
project: visual communication, catalogue
publisher: Centraal Museum
printer: Spinhex, Tuijtel
photography: Daria Scagliola, Stijn Brakkee (bookcover)

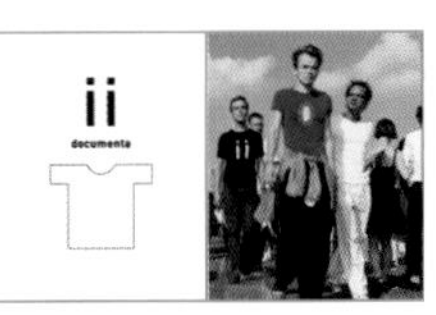

Documenta 11 2000, pp. 38-43
Six agencies from as many countries were invited to compete to design a house style for the 11th Documenta (Kassel, 2002), including Bruce Mau from Canada, Ecce Boonk from Austria and Bureau X from Germany. From the Netherlands, the organisers approached designer collective Droog Design, who invited Studio Gonnissen en Widdershoven, as they were then called, to develop a design.
The theme for the 11th Documenta will be globalization and interdisciplinarity. Globalization: modern art is not just a Western affair. Interdisciplinarity: artists are no longer limited to a single medium; different forms of expression can be used to convey a vision.
Reflecting on the notion of medium and the nature of modern means of communication, we arrived at the T-shirt phenomenon. A T-shirt is a medium, and is worn as such across the world.
As the idea developed, the graphic depiction of a T-shirt on stationary made way for a real T-shirt printed with the letters ii representing the number eleven. Photos from around the world of people wearing the T-shirt would be used on all other house-style items such as book covers, banners, brochures, etc. The house-style project would gradually broaden out, injecting major art event with a new graphic identity. Given the openness of this house-style project, the idea was presented in the form of a book charting the development of the idea. It contained visual essays supporting the premises 'A T-shirt is a medium', 'A T-shirt is global', 'A T-shirt is everybody' and 'A T-shirt is a logo'. Unfortunately the organisers preferred the Austrian proposal.
client: Droog Design for Documenta 11, Renny Ramakers, Gijs Bakker
project: identity programme
photo p. 39: Julika Rudelius
photo p. 40: To Sang
photo pp. 42-43: Bettina Neumann

Burada 2000, pp. 44-45
Advertising agency KesselsKramer thought up the name Burada, meaning 'here', for a major Turkish telecommunications company. The agency commissioned us to produce a logo. We developed

the design in close collaboration with Peter Viksten of KesselsKramer. The name is presented in our favourite letter, Avenir, with the arm of the 'r' replaced by a dot, on which the name appears to pivot.
The simple design was our answer to one of the biggest assignments we ever had; around eighty programmers were waiting to organise Europe's first integrated Internet, television and mobile telecommunications system. A delegation from the two agencies flew to Turkey just before Christmas 2000 to brief them on the new house style. A month later news came that the name had already been claimed as a brand by their rivals. All that remains is the book summarising the idea for the logo.
client: KesselsKramer, Erik Kessels, Peter Viksten and Engine
project: corporate identity

Six and Five Vowels 1999, pp. 46-47
Designer Joost Overbeek invited friends, acquaintances and colleagues to contribute to his magazine 'Het zou me wat worden als iedereen maar gewoon zou doen waar ie zin in had' ('Wouldn't it be something if people just did whatever they wanted?'). At first we thought our contribution should be about sex, but we decided we'd rather focus on vowels. The only limitation was the number of pages: six. So we filled these six with five vowels (sax, sex, six, sox, sux) and a titlepage.
client: Het zou me wat worden als iedereen maar gewoon zou doen waar ie zin in had, Joost Overbeek
project: contribution to the magazine

Architectuur en Verlangen 1999 on, pp. 48-51
ACE occupies a former Philips factory building in Eindhoven called the Witte Dame. It has been completely renovated and restored to its original Neue Sachlichkeit style. The design of the Architectuur en Verlangen exhibition is simple. Twenty-one full-length fold-out boards contain information about the 21 architects. At the front are the 21 letters of the title. Here a prototype inexpensive exhibition is presented in monumental proportions designed to match the space. For those who look more closely, the sides of the boards are in the shape of a letter A, or an inverted V: the initials of the title. These forms also dominate the graphic design of the catalogue cover. The other letters are featured on the following pages, creating not one but six titlepages. We also accentuated the building's architecture in the ACE house style. The logo resembles the plan of a modernist building, yet also shows an exhibition space.
client: Architectuur Centrum Eindhoven, Mariëtte van Stralen
project: identity programme, exhibition design, catalogue
publisher: Thoth Publishers
printer: Spinhex, Veenman
photo pp. 50-51: Arjan Benning

Over the Edges 2000, pp. 52-57
For Over the Edges, a major exhibition by Belgian museum director Jan Hoet, 52 artists produced works of art on the corners of the streets of Ghent. Posters formed the base for the communications programme since these work on the street. A purely typographic

design was chosen and a single colour – red – because that's street language. The poster was dominated by one large character: a capital E. This stood for Edges and is in fact a letter with lots of corners. A white poster, with all the information, formed the basis for four red posters each of which contained part of the information. The E also appeared in house-style items, including commercials, bus stickers, banners and a town map.
client: S.M.A.K., Jan Hoet, Jojanneke Gijsen
project: visual communication, catalogue, tv-commercial
publisher: S.M.A.K.
printer: Van Melle, Spinhex
photo pp. 53, 55, 57: Dirk Pauwels
special thanks to: Lynn Pellens

One size fits all 1997, pp. 58-59
We like standard materials, standard colours and standard formats. In 1997 six books designed by us were featured in that year's exhibition of The Best Book Designs at the Stedelijk Museum Amsterdam: Eternally Yours, N.T.Z.T., Fransje Killaars, Droog Design, Mario ♥ Olimpia and The Best of Wim T. Schippers.
All six are the same size: 17 x 24 cm or precisely half. This format ensures that no paper at all is lost in the production process.

The Best of Wim T. Schippers 1997, pp. 60-63
Wim T. Schippers is an artist who borders consistently on the irritating, while simultaneously – or perhaps as a result – expressing an unprecedented freedom. He is at his best, notes Centraal Museum director Sjarel Ex, when sowing confusion, when not doing what people expect. In this book a minor graphic design problem, the integration of a Dutch and an English text, was resolved with typical Schippers panache. The two languages are superimposed in two colours, red and green, with coloured transparent sheets enclosed to make the respective texts legible. All the illustrations are in red and green duo-tone. A modest, but characteristic selection of his work is presented on loose full-colour plates in a bag at the front of the book – in typical Fluxus style.
client: Centraal Museum, Sjarel Ex, Ranti Tjan
project: catalogue
publisher: Centraal Museum
printer: Snoeck Ducaju
special thanks to: Harry Ruhé and Wim T. Schippers

Fransje Killaars 1997, pp. 64-65
Artist Fransje Killaars works in brightly-coloured textiles. It was fun producing a book for her because she wanted to include actual fabric and because of our shared love of bright colours. It is extremely difficult to incorporate textile into a book in the same way as paper; when cloth is included in a book it is usually pasted in. With the aid of both the printer and the binder we managed to respect the rules associated with book production. Including a piece of fabric like a sheet of paper, forming two pages, required a careful arrangement of the book.
The photo on p. 64 shows Noa and Oskar Billy on a carpet made by Fransje Killaars
client: Galerie de Expeditie
concept: Fransje Killaars

design: Thonik
project: book
publisher: Galerie de Expeditie
printer: Rosbeek
binder: Mathieu Geertsen

Mario ♥ Olimpia 1997, pp. 66-67
The Children's Museum, part of Amsterdam's Tropical Museum, wanted to make a real book about their exhibition on Bolivia. The text reads like a children's novel while dealing with the various educational elements featured in the show. The documentary photos - unusual in a children's storybook - succeed as illustrations to the text thanks to some calculated editing. The interplay of fantasy and reality that represents such a key aspect of Bolivian culture is reflected in the cutout shapes: a coat of feathers is visible through the outline of a plane, suggesting a bird of prey. A glance at the next page reveals the feathers to be part of a bird suit worn by a man in a folklore pageant.
client: Royal Tropical Institute (KIT), Sannette Naeyé, Liesbeth Ruben, Babette van Ogtrop
project: book
publisher: Royal Tropical Institute (KIT)
printer: Rosbeek

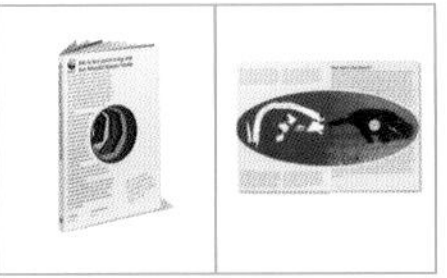

World Wildlife Fund annual report 1995, pp. 68-69
The objective of this annual report was to focus the attention of decision makers – bankers, industrialists and politicians – on the Dutch World Wildlife Fund. The report wanted to express that we can save nature not by doing less but by being smarter. Over the years, the fund's activities have expanded from protection of a few endangered species to a seven-point policy plan. We decided to zoom back in. From abstract objectives to a smart beaver. From the whole wide world to a walk along the riverbank. Each page has a cut-out shape to illustrate the text. This gives the zooming-in a more visible effect. From seven policy points, to six wetlands around the world and five in the Netherlands, to the release of a single beaver. The cost of that one beaver at the end of the annual balance sheet is visible through the cover, at the centre of the cut-outs.
client: Van Lindonk Special Projects – for the Dutch World Wildlife Fund
project: annual report
printer: Bosch en Keuning, Pabo print

Guide to Nature 2000, pp. 70-71
Cor Dera starts his art works with a cut-price nature book. Nothing brings nature as close as a book full of fantastic photos. Dera cuts out all the pictures of the same size in the book and pastes them on mdf before arranging them on a wall.
The book we made with him attempts to demonstrate his fascination as directly as possible. A party of remaindered nature guides was rebound in a new cover designed by the studio; the only additions being an introductory text and a curriculum vitae at the back. And that's how we decided to tackle the tricky question of a book about art–produced–with–books.
The photos on page 70-71 show binder Herman van Waarden rebinding the book.

client: Cor Dera
concept and design: Cor Dera and Thonik
project: book
printer: Spinhex
binder: Van Waarden
photo pp. 70, 71: Julika Rudelius
special thanks to: Herman van Waarden

Archiprix 1996, pp. 72-73
Graduation year at Dutch architectural colleges concludes with an exhibition of the best designs, an award ceremony and a book. Each year a different designer is invited to produce the volume. We were told by the publishers that Archiprix was so well known and enjoyed such guaranteed sales that the cover was not actually needed to attract more buyers. That sounded like a licence to do whatever we pleased. So we decided to treat the cover as an exhibition space and placed work by an artist friend called Frank Mandersloot. As a child he had lived in a small 1950s house built by the famous Dutch architect Gerrit Rietveld. The basement door held a cupboard – to use the space in the small working-class house as efficiently as possible. Frank Mandersloot's work comprised of two photos of this cupboard and a text. We thought it would be fitting to show a photo of this small design by Holland's most famous architect on the cover of this book of grand plans by students.
It took all our powers of persuasion to convince the publishers to take this liberty with the cover. In the end, when the book was finished, hardly anyone noticed its revolutionary aspect.
client: 010 publishers, Hans Oldewarris
project: book
publisher: 010 publishers
printer: Snoeck Ducaju
special thanks to: Frank Mandersloot

The Best Book Designs 1994, pp. 74-75
This catalogue emphasises two characteristics of the book. Firstly, the book as spatial object: the physical aspect expressed in photos of hands holding each volume. The hands are those of the designers who decided their weight and size. After all, a book is made to be held. But the page is also a medium with which to convey information. To give an idea of the pages of the prizewinning books, samples were featured from each volume – for which the original film was used.
Because none of the books featured were the same format or paper as the catalogue, an average size was chosen (17 x 24 cm) and an average type of paper (Bioset). It is a surface on which both fictional texts

When proposing the concept of re-using the original films we simply showed the pages from the 50 best designed books we wanted to reproduce. The client got a little nervous. These were beautiful books, but how was the catalogue going to look they wanted to know. We replied: the same, since we're going to use the original films of all these pages to print the new book.

and art photos feel at home. While the layout of these fifty best books were lost, the legibility of the text and the illustrations were exactly equal to the original.
client: CPNB
project: book, poster
publisher: CPNB
printer: Mart.Spruijt
photography: Gerrit Serné
special thanks to: all the printers for sending us the original films, and all the designers for posing

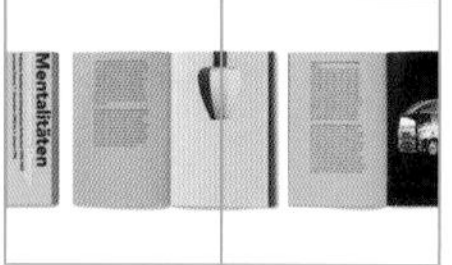

Mentalitäten 1995, pp. 76-77
This catalogue accompanied the Bremen exhibition of 49 products nominated in the previous three years for the Rotterdam Design Prize. During preparations for the show numerous discussions with Christine de Baan, Bart Lootsma and Gert Staal focused on the context in which design products emerge and function. In fact the catalogue theme is 'mentalities instead of objects'. This perspective dictated the presentation of the products in the catalogue.
Traditionally, design products are displayed individually – against the white background of the paper or in the empty space of the photo studio. We wanted to show the objects in a context, and so create a certain interrelation. The catalogue accompanying the Droog & Dutch Design show (Centraal Museum, 2000) features furniture and other utensils displayed in combination with fashion. For a later Droog Design book (Centraal Museum, 1997) Nikki and Thomas placed products in their own home and photographed them there. However, this time it was impossible to have new photos taken of all the objects. So we decided to present them individually, but not against neutral backgrounds.
The settings were chosen at random from a series of 121 mixed colours obtained by combining Pantone 389 green with Pantone violet in cumulative ten-percent doses. Each illustration therefore had an individual serendipitous hue. The colours green and purple were chosen which, when combined, created a neutral black, so that the whole book, including the black-and-white illustrations, could be printed in two colours. The edge of the book is diagonally cut, immediately showing the reader that each page has its own colour. After all, a good cover reveals its contents.
client: de Rotterdamse Designprijs
project: catalogue, poster
publisher: Securitas Galerie
printer: Spinhex
special thanks to: Christine de Baan, Jurgen Bey, Jan Konings, Bart Lootsma, Gert Staal

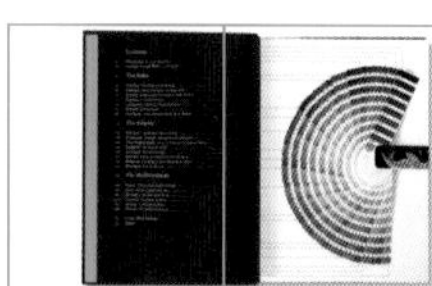

Coast Wise Europe 1997, pp. 78-79
Coast Wise Europe is the joint product of 22 architect courses in as many European coastal countries. Each chapter describes one country's coast, although the various writers do this in different ways. The book is printed and illustrated in full colour. To accentuate both the unity and the diversity, the Pantone full-colour fan was used. Each country was assigned a different colour blue, from purple-blue in the north to green-blue in the south. And in each chapter, tints of these colours are presented in a system of blocks integrating the texts and illustrations.
client: 010 publishers, Peter de Winter
project: book
publisher: 010 publishers
printer: Snoeck Ducaju

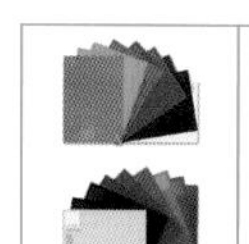

Proton ICA 1994-1995, p. 80
Proton ICA was the small continuation of leading contemporary art exhibition gallery (the ICA) in Amsterdam. It was established in 1994 by Ranti Tjan, currently Head of Presentation at the Centraal Museum in Utrecht. Lack of funds forced the institute to establish its identity clearly. Because it was new and had no permanent residence it was vital that the focus of attention be directed at the institute rather than its temporary exhibitions. The ICA's print work was in yellow on both sides. The front featured a yellow square; on the back it's the square that's left blank. Name and address were added with a simple stamp; the name in the blank square, the temporary address underneath. Invitations to exhibitions were printed in unmixed Pantone colours over the yellow background. The resulting mixed colours were totally random, and not selected to suit the shows advertised.
client: Proton ICA, Ranti Tjan
project: identity programme
printer: Spinhex

Apples & Oranges 2001, p. 81
In 2001 BIS publishers started a series of what they refer to as monographs on young designers and design agencies, of which this volume was the first. At the same time BIS also published the first yearbook of graphic design in the Netherlands, for which editors chose the best designs of the previous year. Because of the arbitrary nature of the exercise we suggested calling the book Apples & Oranges – emphasising the difficulty of making a comparison. Fruit also seemed appropriate since the book was about the graphic designs produced throughout that year. Orange was a reference to the country of origin and to our own studio.
Nikki Gonnissen was invited to be one of the editors and to design it. Together with Gert Staal she proposed dividing the volume into themes instead of the usual alphabetic arrangement, and within the thematic sections she suggested grouping the projects according to characteristics. This approach is unusual for this kind of survey. We reduced the title – relatively long for one of our books – to a pictogram of an orange-coloured apple. All the textual information is on a sticker in the shape of a leaf.
client: BIS Publishers
project: book
publisher: BIS Publishers
printer: Tuijtel
photography: Beerling
special thanks to: the editors, Gert Staal and Ineke Schwartz

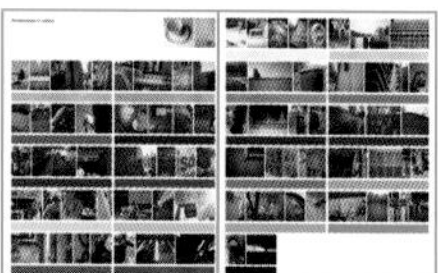

Amsterdam inner-city department annual report
1998, pp. 82-83
Dienst Binnenstad runs a variety of services for government and citizens in Amsterdam's inner city. Several of these activities are highlighted in this annual report,

divided into the visible and invisible services that the department provides. This information is accompanied by a photo essay that focuses on colour in the inner city. Colour is first and foremost visible, but it can also be found in the most surprising places and then only visible through the lens of photographer Bettina Neumann. A meticulous selection of photos charts the whole pallette of the inner city: from white, through grey, blue, purple, red, orange, yellow and green to grey and black.
client: Dienst Binnenstad Amsterdam, Ko van Geemert, Thio Sian-Lie
project: annual report
printer: Tuijtel
photography: Bettina Neumann

Het PAROOL

Big Wil: van onbesproken gedrag, dus gewapend

Opvolgers van Napster staan klaar

Een schoenendoos die nogal in het oog springt

KLM-eis aan fusie Alitalia

Irik wint tegen zin Van der Aa

gezonde slapers

50 jaar in de-kroon

A photo of our new Studio – designed by MVRDV – was featured on the cover of Het Parool. We decided to buy a couple of hundred copies and send them to friends and clients as change of address notice.

Thonik Studio 2001, pp. 84-87
We had the good fortune to find an empty piece of land, in a court yard, in Amsterdam, where we were able to realise our dream: building our own studio. Together with Jacob van Rijs of MVRDV architects and interior designer Richard Hutten we created a space that reflects our view of design. Aaron Betsky, director of the Netherlands Architecture Institute, called it a collaboration of kindred spirits, of people who share the same attitudes in graphic and product design and architecture.
The building is a simple two-storey block. It has an orange exterior of artificial materials that make eaves and sills unnecessary, while windows and doors are formed by seventeen identical French windows.
The first floor rises in four stages. giving the ground floor ceiling different heights. The roof features a tiny swimmingpool and a table-tennis table.
Inside, all the facilities – stairs, toilet, storage – are contained in a single blue volume. Nine oak work tops by Richard Hutten are arranged in the studio which, when linked together, form work islands. For the eighteen-metre blind wall he designed a light-blue item that resembles a battery of kitchen cabinets.
With its orange colour and artificial material the building might easily be mistaken for a model, or an artist's impression. Architectural critic Hans Ibelings described it as 'an idea, life-size '.
client: Thonik
project: our new studio
concept and design: MVRDV, Jacob van Rijs, Eline Strijkers and Bart Spee
interior design: Richard Hutten
contractor: Konst en Van Polen
photo pp. 84, 86, 87: Nicholas Kane
photo p. 85: Julika Rudelius

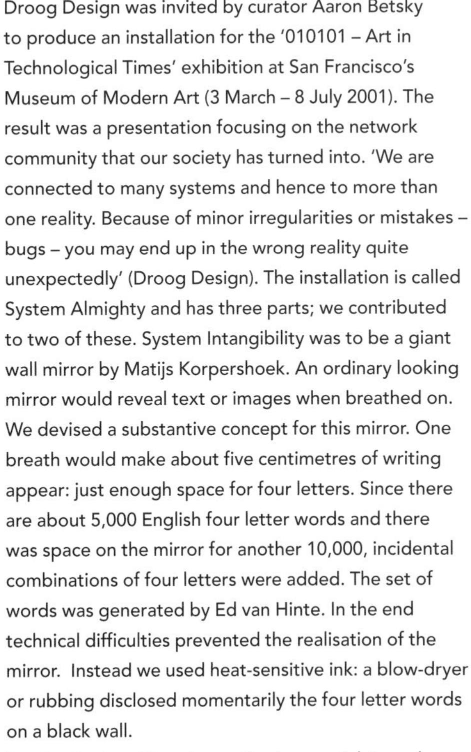

SFMoma installation ('four letr word find f*ck face' and Barcode Scanner) 2001, pp. 88-93
Droog Design was invited by curator Aaron Betsky to produce an installation for the '010101 – Art in Technological Times' exhibition at San Francisco's Museum of Modern Art (3 March – 8 July 2001). The result was a presentation focusing on the network community that our society has turned into. 'We are connected to many systems and hence to more than one reality. Because of minor irregularities or mistakes – bugs – you may end up in the wrong reality quite unexpectedly' (Droog Design). The installation is called System Almighty and has three parts; we contributed to two of these. System Intangibility was to be a giant wall mirror by Matijs Korpershoek. An ordinary looking mirror would reveal text or images when breathed on. We devised a substantive concept for this mirror. One breath would make about five centimetres of writing appear: just enough space for four letters. Since there are about 5,000 English four letter words and there was space on the mirror for another 10,000, incidental combinations of four letters were added. The set of words was generated by Ed van Hinte. In the end technical difficulties prevented the realisation of the mirror. Instead we used heat-sensitive ink: a blow-dryer or rubbing disclosed momentarily the four letter words on a black wall.
For the System Disorder section Lauran Schijven developed a scanner that can read any barcode visitors might have with them. The idea being to allow these random barcodes to cause unique and surprising reactions. We developed the installation together with Ed van Hinte. It is an orange box filled with forty electric products that switch on and off in combinations of four. Apart from ten electric Droog Design products the box also contains thirty ordinary products, including a drill, a vacuum cleaner and an electric train.
client: Droog Design, Renny Ramakers – for SFMoma, Aaron Betsky
project: installation
project participants: Ed van Hinte, Matijs Korpershoek, Lauran Schijvens, Ries Straver and Thonik

oio 2001, pp. 94-95
Rotterdam publishers 010 wanted a new house style. We decided not to create a real logo for two reasons: 010 is itself a powerful image and a publisher's imprint often clashes with the design of the covers on which it appears. We proposed translating the numerals 010 into letters – oio – and then losing the dot on the i. For

some, the image resembles a nose with glasses or an owl. Either way, using letters resulted in an attractive abstract image. The lower case o is rounder than a zero, almost geometrical. Similarly, an i is more symmetrical than a one. Whatever the letter type, the logo is consistently recognisable.
client: 010 publishers
project: identity programme

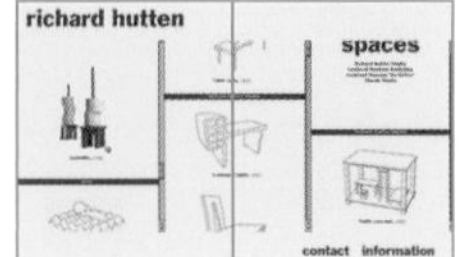

Richard Hutten website 2001, pp. 96-97
After he had furnished our new studio, interior designer Richard Hutten asked us to design his website. All his designs are based on the shape of a table; from the construction of the tabletop on four legs comes the shape of the chairs, cupboard, toilet roll holder and everything else. This simplicity and clarity also characterise his website (www.richardhutten.com). Apart from the full colour photos it uses only two colours: yellow and red. Hutten's designs are divided into three groups: furniture, objects and interiors. Line drawings of these are presented in three columns with successive scroll bars. The drawings focus on the basic form of the design. When the mouse moves over a drawing a photo appears. And since only one photo can be loaded at a time, this hardly takes any time at all.
client: Richard Hutten
project: website (www.richardhutten.com)

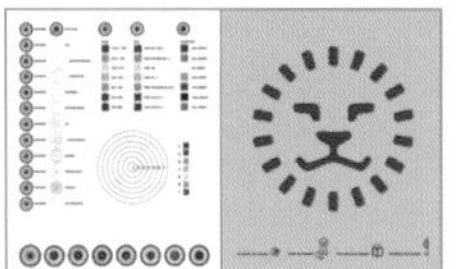

Schorer Foundation 1999, p. 98
The Schorer Foundation is an information centre for gays and lesbians. They asked us for a house style with various logos for the different departments and activities. We felt that this should connect with a generally recognised image. The rainbow is a major symbol in the gay and lesbian world. So we turned the crescent into a full circle, or more accurately, a disc with concentric rings of colours – and at the centre, of course, the foundation. The disc formed the basis for the logos of the various sections of the foundation. For example, the website has a recognisable spiders web motif, and HIV activities are symbolised by a cell. Because money was short, the house style needed to work in black and white as well. In fact the logo is surprisingly effective in grey tones. And with two colours – i.e., one coloured ring and rest grey – the logo is even more striking.
client: Schorerstichting
project: identity programme

Leopold 2001, p. 99
Children's book publisher Leopold asked us to produce a new imprint. Until then they had always had a lion. Because the client had made it abundantly clear that they didn't expect us to suggest a lion, we took especial pleasure in doing just that. It's simply that Leopold is a perfect name for a lion. So we made a childlike and optimistic illustration in an apparently geometrical style. Anything too emphatic would clash with the style of illustrations on the various bookcovers. In fact the dots that form the manes are drawn individually, but with minimal differences. The logo therefore appears symmetrical, but with a lifelike quality.
client: Leopold publishers, Ria Turkenburg
project: identity programme

Init 2001, pp. 100-101
Gert de Graaf of Groosman Partners Architects asked us to help design a façade for a large collective corporate building. He knew about the close collaboration with the architect of our own studio building. What he wanted was an image on the glass façade and on the sunblinds behind the glass which the various occupants of the offices could adapt but that would fit into a single concept. The effect was achieved by introducing a special grid system, a method used by Karel Martens in his book on Wim Crouwel. The dots of colour that make up an image in full colour printing being placed over each other instead of side by side. Close up the effect is strikingly abstract, from a distance the dots form an image. The grid system ensures a strict contrast between the phenomenon seen from the exterior, full of images, and the inside where all that's visible are abstract circles of colour.
client: Groosman Partners Architects, Gert de Graaf – for IBC Vastgoed, Kees Klerks
project: façade

The personal side of graphic design
Studio Gonnissen en Widdershoven had worked for years with a minimal use of materials when simple forms, colours and typography suddenly came into vogue in 1997. These had never formed a style at the studio, just the consequence of an emphasis on the concept: a refusal to allow ideas to be smothered by form. However, we realised that time had caught us up; this method had lost its impact. A reaction was needed: if rigid, impersonal design had become fashionable, now was the time for a more personal approach. Since we always translate our ideas as directly as possible to the form, this resulted in three books featuring the designers themselves. A total volte-face in our approach which was at the same time entirely in line with that approach. And by incorporating pictures of ourselves we managed to solve the basic problem of three highly diverse assignments. For the Raad voor Cultuur (Culture Council) it ensured the required unique and characteristic design; for Eternally Yours it enhanced the connection with the book as industrial product; for Droog Design it solved the problem of how best to present design products. While honouring the particular demands of each of these projects, a network of interconnecting references was also created.
Under the title of 'the personal side of graphic design' the three projects were entered and nominated collectively for the Rotterdam Design Prize. It was the first time that entirely different projects for completely separate clients were submitted as a single project.

Raad voor Cultuur annual report, Droog Design and Eternally Yours

Raad voor Cultuur annual report 1996, pp. 102-105
As design policy advisor, the Raad voor Cultuur (Culture Council) commissions designs from successive new, young designers. We took that policy and developed as original a design as possible for this annual report, thus itself the first realisation of the Raad's policy. Interlinked with the annual report is a photographic account of a journey Nikki and Thomas made that same year to the Asmat people of New Guinea. The two narratives each start with their own front cover and interweave from opposite sides. An opencut cover complements the

titlepage text with the announcement '1996: this year we sought Council from a Culture; here is a report'. A traditional story told by the Asmat people – about a queest for fire – weaves through the photos.
client: Raad voor Cultuur
project: annual report
printer: Spinhex
special thanks to: Roy Villevoye, To-ra-we, Ndo, Antem, Baner, Kaius

Droog Design 1991-1996 1997, pp. 106-109
The design products distributed under the Droog Design label are based on simple but surprising ideas. A chandelier made with a touch of irony, using bare 15 watt bulbs, sockets and wire, for instance. These products are presented equally simply and surprisingly. Designs are usually shown against a neutral, grey background. In our case that would isolate the products, making the ideas and the irony look corny. They are meant to provide highlights in ordinary furnished homes. That's why Nikki and Thomas decided to give them a domestic setting, photographing each one separately in their own home. Blood, sweat and tears accompanying the hoisting of one particularly heavy object; fixing the mirror in the bathroom; the designers engrossed in constructing a bookcase. The idea of getting press photographer Maurice Boyer to take the pictures was Ranti Tjan's. The result is fast, news reporter style photos, rather than slick full-colour photography with shadow.
client: Centraal Museum, Ranti Tjan, Ida van Zijl
project: catalogue
publisher: Centraal Museum
printer: Rosbeek
photography: Maurice Boyer
special thanks to: Maarten Kraanen

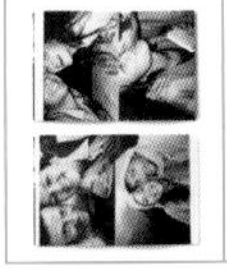

Eternally Yours 1997, pp. 110-112
A series of intimate double portraits of Nikki Gonnissen and Thomas Widdershoven are employed in this volume on sustainable product development as a metaphor for a durable relationship between consumers and their favourite articles. The cover features their first kiss. As a reaction to the title, the book has a 'golden ring' – gilded sides all around. The title is placed on the cut of the book so that it shimmers through the gilded side. The photos of Nikki and Thomas as a couple bear no relation to the content, but together with the gilded sides, the shimmering title and the small format, they make the book something precious – to last forever.
client: Eternally Yours, Ed van Hinte, Arnoud Odding, Liesbeth Bonekamp
project: identity programme, book
publisher: 010 publishers
printer: Snoeck Ducaju

De Volkskrant Opmaat, ADCN invitation card, Postage stamp 1998-1999, pp. 113, 116-117
Our photos featured in three other, smaller projects produced around this time. De Volkskrant asked us to contribute to the front page of Opmaat, the newspaper's weekly cultural supplement. Each issue incorporated the response of an artist or a designer to the supplement's theme; in our case the subject was the

Nikki and Thomas posing with a sandwich board

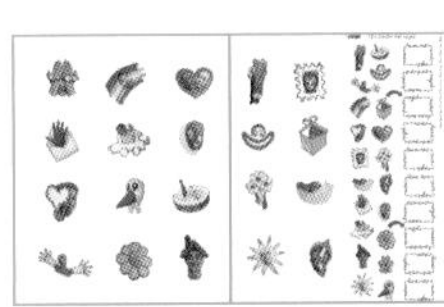

Nikki and Thomas posing for a postage stamp

Nikki and Thomas in the BNO-book

major Escher exhibition. In fact we ignored the formula; the front featured a full-page photo of Thomas and Nikki, then pregnant, on the beach at sunset. We hoped that our free approach to the commission would turn Opmaat's front page into a open podium for artists and designers.
client: De Volkskrant, Opmaat
project: newspaper supplement front page
photography: Joanna Greve
For the Art Directors Club Nederland's annual party we designed a double invitation: for the prize-giving ceremony and for the party itself. The event had a tradition of sending out gimmick invitations, but our design remained sec. Photos of Nikki and Thomas, each with a sandwich board listing the requisite information, appeared on the front and back of the invitation.
client: ADCN
project: invitation card
Our postage stamp plan for the Dutch post office (PTT) marked the conclusion of our 'personal' period. With every ten empty stamps you would get twenty stickers for various 'message moments'. These would feature portraits of Nikki and Thomas disguised as flowers, a cake, a heart and so on. The portraits were made in collaboration with former Dogtroep member Lino Hellings. The proposal did not receive PTT approval, the client insisted on a less theatrical and a less personal design.
client: PTT Post
project: postage stamp
special thanks to: Lino Hellings and Lonneke (make up)

BNO book 1998 and 2000, pp. 114-115, 58-59
We have presented two successive – paid – spreads in this biennial survey produced by the Beroepsorganisatie Nederlandse Ontwerpers (Association of Dutch Designers or BNO). In 1998 we contributed a holiday snapshot of Nikki and Thomas in a French mountain stream. Under the title 'one size fits all' in the 2000 edition we placed a photo of six books designed by us and hailed that year among The Best Book Designs. What is immediately noticeable about these books is that they are all the same standard size.
project: advertisement in BNO book
photography: Marga Scholma

De Balie 2001, pp. 118-119
As a cultural and political centre, De Balie produces a wide range of printed matter. We were asked to impose a sense of unity. Our first assignment for De Balie was the restyling of their monthly events calendar. Normally these were printed in two colours. But printing a batch without text for the next month, and again the next, resulted after three months in an interesting four-colour calendar. The design of the cover is never tied too closely to the monthly theme since it is used for three months in succession. This cut-and-paste aesthetic reflects the speed with which the institution produces its huge volume of printed matter. To avoid any conflict with the existing logo we simply placed the words 'de balie' on the cover. And when they asked us to design a new logo we decided to continue along the same lines, joining the two words together in lower-case Akzidenz Grotesk. This time not in Avenir, since we use it for

another major client, the Centraal Museum. The 'e' of 'de' – the least important letter in the name – is one colour, the other characters another. Emphasising this unimportant letter stresses the symmetry of the 'd' and the 'b', while the name is more easily read as two words. One side effect is that the solitary 'e' is itself developing – pars pro toto – into a logo.
client: de Balie, Eva Groentjes, Andrée van Es
project: identity programme, monthly calendar
printer: de Raddraaier, de Volharding
special thanks to: Alex Clay

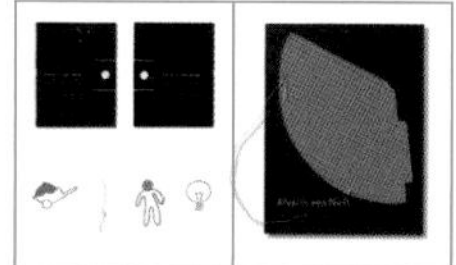

Amsterdam refuse department annual report
1998 on, pp. 120-121
Gemeentelijke Dienst Afvalverwerking incinerates the refuse Amsterdam and the surrounding area produce. That may sound like a dirty job, but the department manages to turn rubbish into plenty of good things. We identified with the infectious enthusiasm of director Daan van der Linden. To avoid repeating the department's long name and unattractive logo on the 1998 annual report cover we decided to project the core message in seven short texts each beginning with 'afval is ...', i.e., 'trash is ...':

- Trash is the start – the department's work begins with trash
- Trash is energy – it's incinerated to produce electricity
- Trash is construction material – what remains is reused
- Trash is money – the department makes a profit
- Trash is work – the department employs a large workforce
- Trash is clean – the department keeps well within the strict environmental norms
- Trash is the end! – that's obvious

The cover of the 1999 annual report contains a removable party hat with the slogan 'trash is a party'. For the department it's a challenge to get as much out of refuse as possible: energy, raw materials, money, employment. That they're succeeding was the reason for the annual report's festive design. Parts of the hat are echoed in the report itself - reused, as it were - in illustrations demonstrating aspects of refuse. A staple represents raw materials and an elastic band recycling.
client: Marje Alleman Creative Projects – for Gemeentelijke Dienst Afvalverwerking, Daan van der Linden, Eveline Jonkhoff
project: annual report, visual communication
printer: Zwaan offset

Sonsbeek 9 2001, pp. 122-127
It was a coincidence that Belgian museum director Jan Hoet saw Nikki Gonnissen's final exam designs at Plaatsmaken publishers in Arnhem. He immediately asked us to take on the visual communication of his major outdoor exhibition, Sonsbeek 9. The assignment was complex: to make it clear that the show features sculpture in public open spaces, that it has a long tradition and that it's no longer confined, as before, to Sonsbeek Park, but now appears in three different locations, the additional sites being Arnhem's historic city centre and a modern shopping mall. The identity we developed features a photo of a naked lower leg in the grass. This reflects the perspective of this year's Sonsbeek, expressed in the subtitle as 'focus on the place, let it inspire you'. The leg in the grass forms a monumental image that builds on the tradition of presenting art surrounded by nature. At the same time it suggests that art is on the move and appearing elsewhere in the city. By placing this image in the folder beside photos of the three locations, the idea of nature is stretched to incorporate the contemporary notion of public space.
Changing the name Sonsbeek 2001 into Sonsbeek 9 was designed to accentuate the history of the event. The numerals 1 to 8 are shown beneath the eight letters of the name Sonsbeek: the roots of this year's exhibition.
client: Sonsbeek 9, Jan Hoet, Hanneke van Tongeren
project: visual communication, catalogue and website
printer: Veenman drukkers
photography: Juul Hondius, Herman van Ommen
special thanks to: Pepijn Zurburg

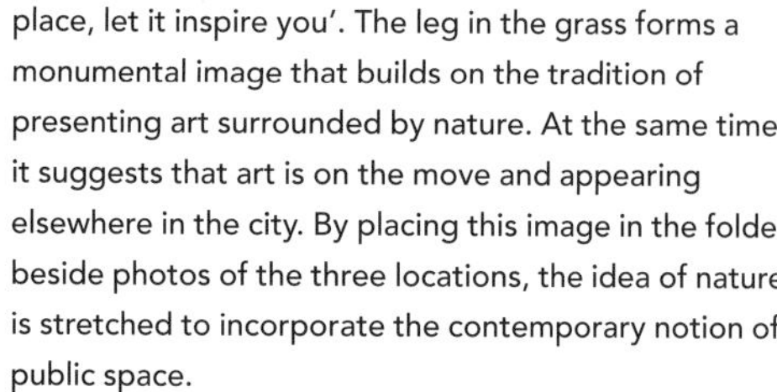

KesselsKramer 96-01 2001, pp. 128-131
A book about the fifty-year career of Amsterdam advertising agency KesselsKramer, producers of campaigns such as Ben, Het Parool and Diesel. After the briefing, the first and hardest problem was the book's cover. Everything KesselsKramer has ever done is so outward-going that it all had to be on the cover. Many of the agency's campaigns would have been ideal as themes for the cover, but also considered were their offices in a church building, the faces of the principal personalities Erik Kessels and Johan Kramer and their name plaque, shaped like a horseshoe. We solved the problem by designing fifty books instead of one. This meant fifty covers. The actual publication is a catalogue of these fifty books. In effect it is a pastiche on the annual catalogue of fifty best designed books that accompanies the Stedelijk Museum's exhibition each year.
client: KesselsKramer, Erik Kessels, Johan Kramer, Joanna van de Zanden
concept: Thonik
design team: Stephan Achterberg, Alex Clay, Rieme Gleijm, Nikki Gonnissen, Yoichi Imai, Alex Nijburg, Thomas Widdershoven, Marieke Zwartenkot
project: book
publisher: BIS Publishers
printer: Kwak & Van Daalen & Ronday
photography: Beerling

Grachtenfestival 2001, pp. 132-133
Following the success of Museum Night, for which we provided the visual communication, we were approached by the organisers of Amsterdam's

Grachtenfestival. This is an annual presentation of classical concerts on and around Amsterdam's canals. It was hoped that our direct approach would attract a younger audience. Although this was accompanied by some reticence: 'We don't want anything as coarse and severe as Museum Night, we want something a little more romantic.' The design had to contain images and associations with classical music and water, and to evoke the theme of passion and fire. After many discussions, a proposal eventually emerged that everyone was completely satisfied with: a simple typographic image of the name.

It is always difficult to cast an existing name in a new form, especially a name like Grachtenfestival. In the end, the length provided the basis for the poster design; since the name was too long for an upright poster, we placed truncated sections on several successive lines, each shifted slightly further along. This ensured that all the letters would appear on the poster and that the whole name would nevertheless be legible. That filled around two-thirds of the poster, a more or less square area. So the bottom third was given a different colour and reserved for the practical details. The continuation of the word Grachtenfestival on both sides of the poster and the intrusion of the light-blue letters over the line dividing the two background colours gives the design a kind of fluid, rippling sense appropriate to a concert on the water.

client: Grachtenfestival, Alma Netten, Gwenoële Trapman
project: visual communication
printer: Spinhex, Mart.Spruijt
photo p. 132: Bettina Neumann
special thanks to: Gerard Jongerius

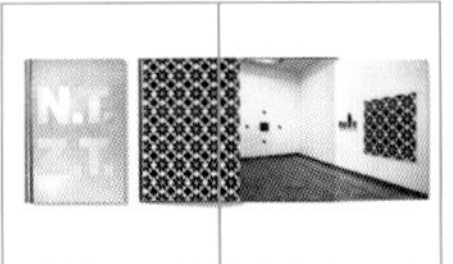

N.T.Z.T. Narcisse Tordoir 1997, pp. 134-135

Narcisse Tordoir's art is at its best in the neutrality of a 1980s gallery or museum. But however clinical the space is, it's still a context. Because the artist is familiar with this setting he is able to manipulate it. A catalogue is a completely different context, however. In this volume we focused, jointly with De Designpolitie, on those aspects of Tordoir's work that would most bring a book to life. Graphic elements from his designs were shown two-dimensionally in the book beside photos of spatial arrangements of his work. So in addition to showing reproductions of the images the book also contains depictions of real situations. The influence of the shifting context is almost tangible as a result.

client: Centraal Museum, Ranti Tjan
concept and design: Thonik and De Designpolitie
project: catalogue
publisher: Centraal Museum
printer: Waanders
special thanks to: Narcisse Tordoir

Ennu 2001, p. 136

Continuing on from 'four letr word' – our concept for the Droog Design installation for '010101' – we subsequently developed four-letter names and titles for a variety of clients. Narcisse Tordoir's untitled exhibition at Centraal Museum had to suffice with an abbreviation: NTZT. This is a relatively abstract typographic image, the Z forming a sideways N. For this fashion company presenting prêt-à-porter garments by leading designers we originally thought of proposing a neutral combination of letters, inspired by unwieldy abbreviations, like company names such as NTU (Nederlandse Tapijt Unie). But then we remembered – or did we dream it? – a painting with two words: 'un' and 'nu', French for 'a nude'. One word on top of the other, like Gary Indiana's painting 'Love'. We had decided that the name had to sound good, and had to suggest a meaning, like the name of the mobile telecommunications company Ben. The term ennu is an ideal vehicle with which to build up a vain, transient, breathless product like fashion – ennu: and now – and now me, and now Commes des Garçons, and now: ennu!

client: Ennu, Pieter Baane
project: name and visual communication
printer: Spinhex
photo: Beerling

un
nu

en
nu

on
no

Onno 2000, p. 137

At the time of the briefing for the design of the Dogtroep theatre company poster the performance still had no name. Dogtroep liked long Latin-American titles. We suggested proposing our own title - which would be the name of the leading character too. Dogtroep wanted the lead role to have a kind of Marlboro Man image; we had something more ambiguous in mind. After all, the play was about identity and the doubts associated with it. The two female roles were opposites, so we suggested calling the women Anna and all the men Onno. That went too far for Dogtroep; they might call the two women Anna, but only the leading man could be Onno. Dogtroep planned to encourage locals to join in as extras; we suggested writing to all the Annas and Onnos in town. That was also rejected. Finally, when Dogtroep began to make extensive changes to the poster and our design for a new logo (in Avenir of course) was rejected it was time for a parting of the ways.

client: Dogtroep
project: name, visual communication
photo p. 138: Julika Rudelius

n8 / 2e n8 2000 and 2001, pp.138, 140-141

When it was realised that www.museumnacht.nl had already been claimed, we decided to make a virtue of necessity. For the logo we proposed using a distinctive style that would establish the Museum Night identity. Text messaging formed the inspiration. After all, many of those taking part in the events would tell each other where they were and what they thought of the activities by text message. 'I'm at the n8w8' Thomas told Nikki during a Nationale Ballet performance at the Rijksmuseum – this abbreviation of Rembrandt's Night Watch employed the Dutch word for eight, 'acht', to spell Nachtwacht. Abbreviating Museum Night to n8 ('nacht') seemed a radical idea. We proposed extending the night from eight to eight, but that was impossible. So there was no inherent reason to explain the use of the figure eight. To enhance the recognisability we decided to produce illustrations in which a celestial body, the beam of a torch or a light-projecting space ship produced a figure eight. Amazingly, the press actually adopted the abbreviation in their reports.

An almost identical logo was used for the second Museum Night, by combining '2e' (second) with 'n8' in a typographic image.
client: Museum Night Amsterdam, Joke Bosch, Daniël Bouw, Caroline Bunnig, Joost Milde, Sandra Malaver, Kwinten Vissers, Sander Kos
project: name, visual communication
printer: Mercurius, Tuijtel
image editing: Neroc
photo p. 141: Bettina Neumann

1ab 2002, p. 139
The theme of the first Architecture Biennial Rotterdam is 'mobility'. What place does a building, a site, a city have in a world in which everything – people, goods, data – are continually on the move? A question to which the numerous events, exhibitions and lectures organised for the biennial will hopefully produce an answer. We had already reformulated Museum Night into n8.
With its long name we felt that the Eerste Architectuur Biënnale was in even greater need of a short, sharp image. We came up with 1ab, again a combination of numbers and letters. And again in Helvetica, which is even simpler than our house lettertype, Avenir.
1ab is reminiscent of signs, of road numbers on motorways and of station platform numbers, linking in turn to the event's theme. To emphasise this we added an arrow. It points in a different direction on each house-style item and turns like a compass needle on the website. By including the numeral 1 in the design – which coincidentally echoes the initials of its director Aaron Betsky – we built in a kind of counter. The result is a house style that generates a unique image for each successive event while remaining recognisable.
client: 1ab, Aaron Betsky, Wim Noordzij, Angela van der Heijden
project: name, visual communication
printer: Tuijtel
special thanks to: Kristin Feireiss

Made in Japan, Centraal Museum 2001, pp. 142-143
In addition to the catalogue and the poster, the Centraal Museum invited us to design the presentation of an exhibition of contemporary classical and avant-garde fashion from Japan. For the ennu project we had attended various spring fashion shows in Paris, from which we developed the idea of basing the design on a catwalk. We then turned the functions of the stage and the room around; visitors to the exhibition would walk down the white, brightly-lit catwalk passing costumed dummies in the dark rooms. The costumes would be mysteriously lit by the reflected light. An additional advantage was the avoidance of damaging direct light on the fabric. And the public felt like stars.
client: Centraal Museum, José Teunissen, Erica van Buchem
project: exhibition design, poster, catalogue
publisher: Centraal Museum
printer: Tuijtel
photography: Maurice Boyer and others
photo p. 142: Ernst Moritz

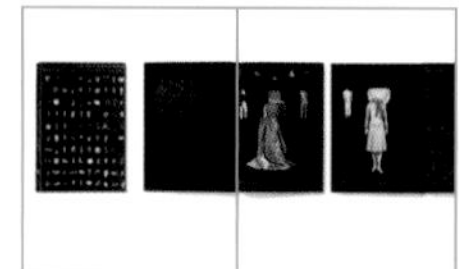

Droog & Dutch Design 2000, pp. 144-145
We generally try to present products in some kind of context in our design books. In a previous Droog Design book we photographed their furniture in our own house. For this catalogue accompanying a combined exhibition of Dutch fashion and Droog Design at the Centraal Museum, we took a different approach. Droog Design products have become icons of Dutch design, and we wanted to present them as such. For the fashion illustrations we had no context to show. José Teunissen, curator of the museum's leading fashion collection, has a neutral pictorial inventory of all the designs. Instead of photographing the garments specially for the catalogue we had to make do with photos of clothes on tailor's dummies. Any remaining context was simply cut away.
We placed all one hundred Droog Design and fashion items on the cover against a black background. And each object was placed completely at random in this field of ten-by-ten pictures. The book was aimed principally at the Japanese market. It seems that the Japanese still have a problem with perspective, as developed in Europe in the fifteenth century.
So although we may not consider perspective to be the most exciting contribution European culture has ever made, we decided it would be an appropriate way of presenting European design. While the objects were shown in a flat grid on the cover, inside each item was portrayed from a bird's-eye view, with the other objects behind, diminishing in size. Five different perspectives were featured: each object being presented from an angle best suited to that item.
client: Centraal Museum, José Teunissen
project: catalogue
publisher: Centraal Museum
printer: Tuijtel
photography: Maartje Geels, Hans Wilschut, Dea Rijper

Société Gavigniès 2000, pp. 146-147
Société Gavigniès is the only client who came to us through our 'advert' in the BNO yearbook of 1998/1999 featuring a photo of Nikki and Thomas paddling in a

French mountain stream. The Société supervises the legacy of pianist Madeleine Margot, who died enormously rich, but unmarried and childless. She left her fortune to a trust fund to promote classical music. This was named after a cello by the instrument maker François Gavigniès, which Margot had once bought with her lover. The Société asked us to design a logo and produce the layout for a book on the life of the pianist. We placed the last two letters of Gavigniès in front of the first letter. This resulted in a logo which when read aloud sounds like SG: Société Gavigniès; ès and G are musical notes, it is a combination that's often heard and has an optimistic sound. Fragments of music in which this combination occurs are featured on the fund's website. Grey, cyan and a mixture of these two form the house-style colours. These were augmented with silver in the book 'De hoge lucht: Het leven van Madeleine Margot (1902-1997)'. The illustrations are depicted in various combinations of grey, cyan and silver.

client: Société Gavigniès, Renee Jonker, Henriëtte Post
project: identity programme, book, website (www.gavignies.com)
publisher: Thoth Publishers
printer: Mart.Spruijt, Spinhex
binder: Van Waarden

T-shirt pendant 2000, p. 148

This pendant was made during the project for documenta 11, in collaboration with Dinie Besems. The pendant has not found a manufactorer to date.

client: own initiative
photo p. 148: Julika Rudelius
special thanks to: Dinie Besems

Tirade 1996 on, p. 149

George Moormann of poetry magazine De Zingende Zaag was appointed to edit the established literary periodical Tirade in 1996. Having previously worked for De Zingende Zaag, we were approached by Moormann to produce designs for Tirade. The covers are purely typographical. For each issue, the editors choose a thematic quotation. We use this as the basis for an apposite image.

client: Tirade, George Moormann
project: literary magazine covers
publisher: Van Oorschot

Basta 1998, 1999, 2000, p. 150

Each issue contains an incredible number of names and a store of information about contemporary art in the Netherlands in the year covered. A book of lists, lists and more lists. To make these volumes more accessible and a little more exciting, they are sometimes printed in colour, with a spot colour. In the first issue these were the subject of an autonomous experiment. They were printed using the split-colour method. The main colour progressed from blue, to purple, to red; the complementary spot colour from orange, to yellow, to green.
Theoretically, each of these combinations should produce black when superimposed. However, split-colour printing is not a precise process, and offset inks don't always behave predictably. To show how the results differ in practice each page had a bar in which grids of colour and spot colour overlapped 50 per cent. In theory, this should have produced a neutral grey, but the actual colour varies from dark grey to salmon pink. The page featuring Centraal Museum director Sjarel Ex's foreword – printed entirely in this 'grey' – turned out to be perhaps the most attractive in the book.
The cover, with a silkscreen title in powdery relief, was developed by textile designer Eugène van Veldhoven.

client: Centraal Museum, Ranti Tjan
project: books
publisher: Centraal Museum
printer: Spinhex
special thanks to: Klaas van der Veen, Eugène van Veldhoven

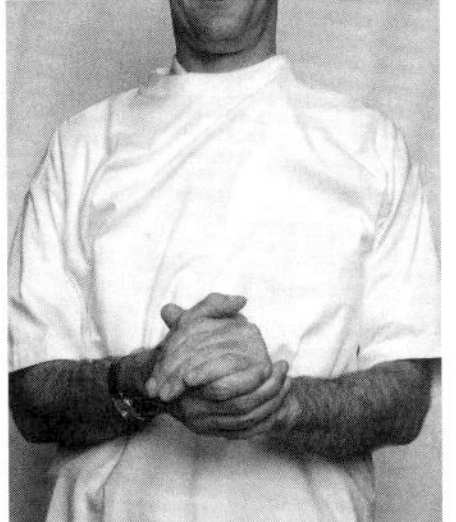

Cultuurnota 2001-2004: Culture as Confrontation
2000, p. 151

In this political document the Dutch secretary of state for culture, Rick van der Ploeg, summarised his policy for the coming four years. Thonik were given plenty of leeway in the design, remarkably for a government policy statement. They interpreted the emphasis on cultural minorities and the general public in a series of portraits of hands that appear to clap when flitting quickly through the pages. Is this music, or is it applause? Or is it – ironically – applause for the statement? Like an animation book the volume is thick and small. It resembles a Bible, which is appropriate perhaps for a book that subsidy candidates study meticulously.

client: Ministerie van OCenW (Ministry of education, culture and science), Rick van der Ploeg, Gitta Luiten
project: Cultuurnota
printer: SDU
photography: Juul Hondius

That was some party 1998, pp. 164-165

These photos were taken at the opening of our former studio which we shared with fellow designers De Designpolitie. We wanted our photo taken with everyone at the party, but we knew it would be impossible to keep smiling all the time. So we asked everyone to pose beside a life-size cardboard photo of ourselves. When someone suggested compiling a book of the photos, printer Cor Rosbeek spontaneously offered his services. The volume was later sent as a souvenir to everyone who had been there.

client: own initiative
concept and design: Thonik and De Designpolitie
project: book
printer: Rosbeek
photography: Gerrit Serné
special thanks to: Cor Rosbeek and Gerrit Serné

Thank You / That was some party

Thanks to our mentors, especially
Elisabeth Gonnissen, George Moormann, Kees Ruyter, Ranti Tjan, Roy Villevoye

Thanks to our family, especially
Elisabeth, Julia and Stephan Gonnissen

Colette and Jan Gijsen, Guy and Emilie Widdershoven, Guy, Ton-Peter Widdershoven, Marie-Ange Zervakis, Raymond, Cyril, Philippe Gijsen, Suzanne Weyers Noëlle Widdershoven, Ronald Widdershoven

Thanks to Thonik
Alex Nijburg, Tijs Bonekamp, Phebe Kemper, Sven Sörensen, Eva Grinder, Rieme Gleijm, Marieke Zwartenkot, Martijn Engelbregt, Marianne de Vrijer

Thanks to all the people who help us, especially
Carla Spaansen, Gijs Verloop, Robin Hulsbergen

Thanks to our interns, especially
Stefan Achterberg, Yoichi Imai, Alexandra Noth, Debbie Saul, Maartje de Sonnaville

Thanks to the authors of this book
Ed van Hinte, Ineke Schwartz and Gert Staal

Thanks to our friends, especially
Joanna Greve and Frans Hempen, Oskar Billy, Astrid Vlug and Philibert Schogt, Karolien Knols and Irminia Lentjes, Ruud Douma, Marga Scholma and Haico Beukers, Tirso Francès, Ron Faas, Richard and Femke van der Laken, Pepijn Zurburg, Seda Angenent Guido Pouw, Ilga Dekker and Michael Buchenauer, Esther Rouhard and Raymond Debats

Thanks to our friends and colleagues, especially
Jurgen Bey, Sybren Kuiper, Joost Overbeek, Pieter Roozen, Jacques Koeweiden, Paul Postma, Robert-Jaap Jansen, Klaas van der Veen, Marianne van Ham, Mart Warmerdam, Erik Kessels, Ewald Spieker, Hans Wolff, Greet Egbers, Harmen Liemburg, Richard Niessen, Edwin Vollebergh, Petra Janssen, Thomas Buxo, Jan Konings, Irma Boom, Vincent van Baar, Ewan Lentjes, Daniël van der Velden, Herman van Bostelen, Peik Suyling, Reinoud Homan, Martin Majoor, Roelof Mulder, Rick Vermeulen, Cor van Wees, Lex Reitsma, Eugène van Veldhoven, Mieke Gerritzen, Rick Verhoog, Wil Holder, René Put, Pieter Vos, Arjen Groot

Thanks to the masters of Dutch Design, especially
Wim Crouwel, Anthon Beeke, Ben Bos, Karel Martens, Dick Bruna, Bram de Does

Thanks to the artists and friends we worked with, especially
Frank Mandersloot, Dinie Besems, Moritz Ebinger, Karolien Berkenbosch, Luuk Wilmering, Annemarie Nibbering, Fransje Killaars, Cor Dera, Hans van Koolwijk, Marije van der Hoeven, Wim T. Schippers, Mathilde ter Heijne, Narcisse Tordoir, Lino Hellings, Lauran Schijven

Thanks to everybody at the Centraal Museum, especially Sjarel Ex, Milou Halbesma, Ida van Zijl

Thanks to Jan Hoet and all his teams, especially Jojanneke Gijsen

Thanks to Droog Design, especially Renny Ramakers, Gijs Bakker

Thanks to all the poets and artists we worked with for De Zingende Zaag, especially Harry Mesterom, Marinus Pütz, Toine Moerbeek, Mirko Krabbé, Anke Akerboom and special thanks to Peter Kok

Thanks to the clients and friends we worked for and with, especially Liesbeth Schouten, Hans Oldewarris, Peter de Winter, Rick van der Ploeg, Gitta Luiten, Eva Groentjes, Andrée van Es, Joke Bosch, Daniël Bouw, Paul Mertz, Marje Alleman, Daan van der Linden, Eveline Jonkhoff, Madeleine van Lennep, Ria Turkenburg, Renee Jonker, Henriëtte Post, Gerbrand Borgdorff, Ko van Geemert, Thio Sian-Lie, Ryer Kras, Gert de Graaf, Kees Klerks, Bart Lootsma, Mariëtte van Stralen, Tom Nauta, Tiny and Piet Jongerius, Henk-Jan Gortzak, Pieter Baane, Alma Netten, Wim Noordzij, José Teunissen, Kristin Feireiss, Christine de Baan, Johan Kramer, Joanna van der Zanden, Desmond Spruijt, Sannette Naeyé, Bob Malmberg, Matti Veltkamp, Ada Lopes Cardozo, Marie Hélène Cornips, Julius Vermeulen

Thanks to all photographers and friends we worked with, especially Maurice Boyer, Gerrit Serné, Julika Rudelius, Bettina Neumann, Juul Hondius, Arjan Benning, Hans van der Meer

Thanks to all printers we worked with, especially Jos Hexspoor, Erik Wink, Cor Rosbeek

Thanks to all binders we worked with, especially Herman Van Waarden, Mathieu Geertsen

Thanks to Thomas's fellow teachers at HKA, especially Rein Houkes

Thanks to all our students

Thanks to all our teachers, especially Gerard Unger, Joke Roobaard, Tineke Stevens

Thanks to those who wrote about us, especially Max Bruinsma, Peter Hall, Hub Hubben, Marina de Vries, Hester Wolters

Thanks to those who included us in their exhibitions, especially Aaron Betsky, Peter Bilák, Adam Eeuwens, Tomoko Sakamoto, Almar Seinen

Thanks to everybody connected to our Asmat trip, especially Piet van Mensvoort, Vince Cole, To-ra-we, Ndo, Antem, Baner, Kaius, Aimanam

Thanks to the designers and builders of our studio, especially Jacob van Rijs, Bart Spee, Eline Strijkers, Richard Hutten, Ruud Kolijn

Thanks to our neighbours and friends, especially Liz Cornelissen, Phil van Velzen, Michaël Ferron, Emiel Geugjes

Many thanks to everybody at BIS Publishers, especially Rudolf van Wezel, Willemijn de Jonge

Many thanks to everybody at Tuijtel, especially Erik Wink

Thonik are: from left to right, bottom; Thomas Widdershoven, Eva Grinder, Alex Nijburg, Phebe Kemper, Noa top; Nikki Gonnissen, Tijs Bonekamp, Rieme Gleijm, Sven Sörensen

Thonik are

Apart from founders Nikki Gonnissen and Thomas Widdershoven, there are a number of skilled and talented individuals without whom there would be no Thonik.

At times of high pressure – which are not so seldom – we are very fortunate to have someone with Alex Nijburg's professional expertise and personal calm on the team. Alex is our trusted systems manager and his excellent desktop publishing skills have safely guided us through many major projects, notably the corporate identities for Centraal Museum and De Balie, and the Over the Edges and Sonsbeek events.

Tijs Bonekamp studied at the Arnhem Academy of Arts and Design (where Thomas teaches on a regular basis). At the studio, he has quickly outgrown his 'former student' status, combining a gutsy attitude with a keen eye for the right design in the right place. We blindly rely on Tijs to prove that our designs translate wonderfully into web sites. In addition, he has created a number of readily-identifyable Thonik sites from scratch, such as richardhutten.com and thonik.nl.

As our office manager, Phebe Kemper is Thonik's ambassador to the outside world. Knowing that she makes sure everything runs smoothly is a great reassurance to us. Phebe has played a crucial role in increasing the level of professionalism at our studio. Moreover, she raises everyone's spirits with her excellent lunches, always a welcome sight for eyes sore from staring at computer screens.

Take a Swedish designer, train her in London, turn her loose in an orange building, and what do you get? Why, the epitome of Dutch design. If there is anybody at our studio who creates trademark Thonik designs, it is Eva Grinder. She has worked on several books and corporate identities. We have seen living proof that such a thing as design chemistry exists in the concept for the second n8 that Eva developed with Tijs.

We first worked together with Sven Sörensen on the catalogue for Sonsbeek 9, which he co-ordinated and edited while on the client's team. Sven has only recently become a member of Thonik's team, yet he has already made his mark, putting tremendous effort into writing the project descriptions for this book. He is a real asset to our studio in his capacity as a production manager and copy editor for Thonik.

After several previous internships at other Dutch studios, Rieme Gleijm applied for a place at Thonik. She was closely involved with the award-winning Panorama 2000 catalogue. We offered Rieme a position on our design team, but she opted to train for two more years, at the Royal College of Art in London. We stayed in touch and are thrilled to have her back at Thonik.

Marieke Zwartenkot came to Thonik at a time when the studio was making the exciting step from 'just the two of us' to building a creative team. She helped develop our sense of our own style on various trademark Thonik projects, such as the book for KesselsKramer. In addition, the Amsterdam in Colour project and the corporate identity of the Schorer Foundation bear her signature. Marieke currently works as an independent designer.

Marianne de Vrijer came to Thonik as a former student of Thomas. During her nine months at the studio, she contributed a wealth of ideas and worked on numerous projects. We are particularly happy with the work she did on the corporate identity for Leopold and on two books for the Centraal Museum. Marianne now works as an independent designer.

Designer/artist Martijn Engelbregt worked at Thonik for six months. As senior designer he absolutely rose to the occasion during the move to our new building, even though he was only working on a part-time basis. Martijn's contribution to the Grachtenfestival and his powerful designs for several catalogues, including Sonsbeek 9 and Made in Japan, are among our favourites. Martijn now focuses on his own art (EGBG) and design activities.

About the authors

In the 1970s Ed van Hinte studied aviation and space technology for two years before switching to Industrial Design at Delft Technological University. He graduated in 1981 on ergonomic and semantic research into the relation between shape and use. Since 1980 he has worked as a freelance journalist for various magazines concerned with industrial design, focusing on technology, ergonomics, methodology and environment. In 1989 he was appointed editor of Industrieel Ontwerpen which later merged with Items. At present Ed van Hinte writes for Kunststof Magazine, Het Parool, Polytechnisch Tijdschrift and is editor of Items. In 1996 he won the Jan Bart Klaster Award for art criticism.

Ineke Schwartz (b. 1961) is a freelance art critic. Apart from writing for books, magazines, newspapers and the Internet she presents and makes programmes for television, live debates and the Internet. Her main interest is the connections between art, culture and developments in society. Seeing the Eternally Yours book in 1997 she fell in love with Thonik's work and included it a year later in a special about Dutch Design for Elsevier Magazine. She met Thomas and Nikki for the first time in 1999.

Gert Staal (b. 1956) is writer and editor at Staal & de Rijk / Editors in Amsterdam since 2000. He is, among other things, chief editor of Items, a bimonthly magazine on design and visual culture. He is also attached to the graphic design department of St Joost Academy in Breda. While assistant director of the Design Institute he was involved in editing the Mentalitäten catalogue, his first co-production with Thonik in 1996. More recent collaborations include Boris en de Paraplu - Sketchbook (Centraal Museum Utrecht, 2000) and the annual review of Dutch graphic design, Apples & Oranges (BIS Publishers, 2001).

Selected bibliography

Apples & Oranges 01: Best Dutch Graphic Design, BIS Publishers, 2001

HD: Holland Design new graphics, exhibition catalogue Barcelona, Actar, 2001

New Design: Amsterdam, the edge of graphic design, Rockport Publishers Inc., 2001, p. 176 ff.

Judith Witte; De voet in een bijzonder daglicht, Podopost, no. 7, September 2001, p. 13

Peter van Kester; Achter de oranje gevel van Thonik, Items, no. 2, May/June 2001, p. 44 ff.

Marina de Vries; Een schoenendoos die nogal in het oog springt, Het Parool, 13 February 2001

Reclame Jaarboek, Art Directors Club Nederland, 1995, 1997, 1998, 1999, 2000

Stef van Breugel; The visual age: Dutch design is synonymous with the new Dutch Modernism, Dutch, no. 28, July/August 2000

Catalogus Best Verzorgde Boeken, CPNB, 1993, 1994, 1995, 1996, 1997, 1999

Kees Broos, Paul Hefting; Grafische vormgeving in Nederland. Een eeuw, V+K Publishing, 3rd revised edition, 1999, p. 214 ff.

Graphic Design in the Netherlands: The New Edition of Design Exchange, China Youth Press, China, no. 13, 1999, p. 104 ff.

Toon Lauwen, Almar Seinen; Mooi maar goed: Grafisch ontwerpen in Nederland 1987 - 1998, exhibition catalogue Amsterdam, Paris and Barcelona, Stedelijk Museum Amsterdam, 1999

Robert Thiemann; Immagini Nascoste (Hidden Images), Rinterni, La Rivista Dell'Arredamento, no. 496, December 1999, p. 160

Hub Hubben; Wij houden van gewoon papier, gewone letters: Boekenjury bekroont degelijk en onleesbaar ontwerp, De Volkskrant, October 10, 1998, p. 11

Ineke Schwartz; Dutch Design, Elsevier Magazine, no. 38, September 1998, p. 134 ff.

Peter Hall; Eternally Yours, The International Design Magazine, July/August 1998, p. 120

Do Normal: Recent Dutch Design, exhibition catalogue, San Francisco Museum of Modern Art, 1998

Rineke van Houten; Gonnissen en Widdershoven zetten zichzelf in hun ontwerp, Items, no. 17, March 1998, p. 22 ff.

Ida van Zijl; Droog Design 1991-1996, Centraal Museum, 1997, p. 128 ff

Fred Vermeulen; Componeren van kaft tot kaft, Blad, no. 10, May 1997, p. 37 ff.

Mentalitäten: Niederländisches Design, exhibition catalogue, Securitas Galerie, Bremen, Germany, 1996

Karel Kuitenbrouwer; The New Sobriety, Eye, 1996

Max Bruinsma; De zingende zaag, Items, no. 2, April 1994

Colophon

Publisher BIS Publishers, Amsterdam

Design Thonik® (www.thonik.nl)

Texts Ed van Hinte, Ineke Schwartz, Gert Staal

Translations Sam Herman, Amsterdam

Photography books Beerling, Amsterdam

Lithography and printing Grafisch Bedrijf Tuijtel, Hardinxveld-Giessendam

Binding Callenbach, Nijkerk